HANDS OFF COCKS
HANDS ON SOCKS

IN THE SERVICE OF THE NATION

By Lindlay Nelson

Grosvenor House
Publishing Limited

The right of Lindlay Nelson to be identified as the author of this
work has been asserted in accordance with Section 78
of the Copyright, Designs and Patents Act 1988

This book is published by
Grosvenor House Publishing Ltd
Link House
140 The Broadway, Tolworth, Surrey, KT6 7HT.
www.grosvenorhousepublishing.co.uk

A CIP record for this book
is available from the British Library

ISBN 978-1-78623-114-7

This story is dedicated to my wife Barbara, and son Conrad, the encouragement of both having motivated me throughout its writing.

Chapter 1

HANDS OFF... HAGGIS

It was hot, but I shivered. I took two puffs of my Bon Accord inhaler, held my breath to a count of twenty, then stepped out of the curtained cubical carrying my clothes in a cotton bag. In front of me was a very large room full of naked young men; some, to judge by their hairiness, were not so young.

Oh GOD! I thought (and me a non-believer) *am I to join them?* I knew I had to, but I didn't want to. Because I was an only child, I never had to share a bath with a brother or sister. I had always felt awkward, naked, in the company of other nude males, in the showers after football and in the showers at school after swimming.

This room, with its bare oak floor, very high ceiling, neon lighting, tables covered in instruments, nude youths of all shapes and sizes, nurses and doctors, was my idea of hell. Warmth and sweaty humidity arose from all the bodies. The nudes, some startlingly white all over like myself, some brown with white backsides, one or two brown all over, were being herded by nurses into lines for examination. Most of the nurses were

1

matronly, but to my horror I noticed a few as young as me, making me feel even more inhibited in my nudity.

Standing there I was aware of my bare feet on the wooden floor. I had difficulty swallowing and could not move; a motherly nurse with a kind face took me by the arm and joined me onto a line of mainly white naked-ness worming its way towards doctors, stethoscopes, rubber hammers, weighing and measuring machines. I tried to keep my distance from the lad in front of me, who was as fat as I was skinny. He appeared to be even more fearful than me, and was sweating profusely.

On arrival at the doctors, chests and backs were sounded. We were then taken aside and sat on a chair to have our reflexes tested with rubber hammers. I relaxed here, and was even amused at my legs jerking forward at the hammer taps. I was pushed onto a scale, weighing in at 8 stone 7 lbs and then placed under a height device. I felt the bar was brought down on my head with unnec-essary violence, the weary misanthropic nurse barking "five foot eight" to a sonsy nurse who gave me a wink.

Oh please God (again) *not an erection!* - They were easy to come by in those days. A nurse came up, asked that I open my mouth, roughly forced my tongue down with an object like a stainless steel spoon, and shone a torch down my throat. I gagged which was ignored. She made some quick notes on a pad, then ushered me on to another nurse who had me touch my toes. The fat boy in front of me had farted on doing this but in those days I never farted involuntarily. Toes touched, I then had to pick up a pencil with them. Noting that I didn't have flat feet, the nurse then moved me to a wizened old doctor who avoided my eyes as he weighed my testicles in his cold bony hand.

"Cough!" he said. I coughed. "Again!" he said.

Is he enjoying this? I thought. The result recorded, I was then moved towards the large windows at the end of the room. Here a line of bare backs were peeing into test tubes and surreptitiously evaluating each other's manhood. A large mature male stepped back from the line, drying his penis on a piece of toilet paper provided for that purpose. Not at all embarrassed by his nakedness, he smiled as he handed a named and dated phial, full of straw coloured liquid, to a nurse. A young, pretty nurse (I was embarrassed again) handed me an empty phial and pushed me into the empty window place. I found myself in a row of guys in front of the window looking down onto the pedestrians passing way below in Bothwell Street. A waist-high curtain gave privacy, not that any pedestrian was looking up. At first I couldn't pee and then I couldn't stop. The phial overflowed into the bowl provided for such an occurrence. I wiped myself, added my name and date on the slip provided, and hurriedly handed the lot back to the young nurse. She smiled, grabbed the overflow bowl and departed quickly to the nearby toilet. I then picked up my sack of clothes, found a vacant cubical, got dressed and came out. New embarrassed youths were arriving, aghast like I had been, at what they saw in front of them. I gave them a smile, and the complacent nod of someone who had come through Hades with equanimity. I bounded joyfully down the stairs of the wally close, three at a time and rushed out into the fresh air, space, and clothed wayfarers of Bothwell Street. My medical for National Service had been accomplished.

One week later I had a letter telling me I had passed A1. A1 indeed; not bad for a lifetime asthmatic. The letter said I'd be receiving my calling up papers in about 10 days. I waited with anticipation as this was my chance to break out into the big world. I wanted to get away from my childhood places and my work as a stockbrokers' clerk; it was well paid, but boring. I wanted to travel and see a bit of the world. I imagined that National Service would do that for me.

I waited. Some of my pals got their papers but I didn't. This was a manhood thing; they were going - they were men now, no longer teenagers. I wasn't going; I was being left behind - I was still a teenager. I felt humiliated, but I went out with them for a farewell drink. They were excited, and looking forward to a new experience. I wasn't and I was depressed. I'd passed A1, yet some of them hadn't. Ian and Billy were going into the Army. Alastair, 6ft 2in and 5th in last year's British Boys Golf Championship, had flat feet; he was no good to the Army so he was going into the Air Force. I felt they were thinking, 'Oh Lindlay, asthmatic and always off school; he'll be no use to the Forces'. I saw them off home, went home myself, and lamented my unhappiness non-stop to my grandparents.

My granny was a lovely cuddly wee woman. She had sidelined her encroaching rheumatism to nurse me through my ailments. She and my grandpa had taken over my upbringing from my errant father, who had avoided marrying my 17 year old mother. They had taken on a lot, for although the doctor at my birth had announced me to be a 'healthy hearty bairn', I had developed asthma and an allergy to eggs a few years later. This meant trying times for my grandparents, trying to alleviate my breathing difficulties, and to guard me from egg bearing dishes. In the days before the NHS it was also expensive for my treatment and medicine. My grandfather was unemployed until just before World War II, so money was scarce. My father was working as a salesman for the Daily Express until the war, when he found himself a reserved job in the Auxiliary Fire Service. He may have helped; I never knew.

My granny was a great cook and built up a library of non-egg dishes for my benefit. She made me delicious suet dumplings for my mince and tatties, and her 'clootie dumplings' were one of the great events of my childhood. I was fascinated by the way she moulded the flour, fruit, milk and water, and lucky sixpences for lucky eaters, into a pumpkin shape, retained in a large clean cotton cloth. This she lowered gently, for it was heavy, into a big pot for several hours of steaming. An old flat iron was put on the lid to control the James Watt effect. As it cooked, mouth-watering aromas wafted through the house. After several hours of topping up the water, she carefully took it out, swollen and heavy in its cloth, giving off steam and delicious fruity cinnamon smells. She placed it in front of the open fire to dry off. The outside took on a delightful shiny light leathery skin that guarded the moisture of the fruity, cinnamon interior. It smelt divine, looked lovely, and kept me and the rest of the family in dumpling treats. Wedges were eaten new while still hot, reheated with milk or cream for pudding, or toasted for breakfast; it was a week's delicious eating from one dumpling.

My granny was a loving woman and always did her best for me. I loved her, but I was nasty to her. When she finally broke down under my constant lamenting of rejection, she admitted that she had written to the War Office to tell them that due to my asthma, I wasn't fit for National Service. Hence no calling up papers. I shouted and raged that she and my grandpa were determined that I was not to see the world outside the west of Scotland; that I was to be treated as an asthmatic invalid all my life. Me who had passed my medical A1, and wasn't going anywhere, because of THEM. Me, whose pals would be looking upon me as a weakling for the rest of my life, because of THEM. I accused THEM of preventing me from doing what I wanted to do, of ruining my life. To this day I am ashamed of how I behaved to the grandparents who had done so much for me, who had put me at the centre of their lives. In my grandmother's case it was to the detriment of her own health.

Two weeks later I received the call to go for a second medical at the same place, Bothwell Street. This time I knew the score and didn't have the previous apprehension and timidity about my nudity. It was the same routine as before and again I came away feeling I had done all right. I had. A letter came telling me that once again I had passed A1. I was very pleased to be certified twice, fitter than I ever thought I was.

My granny was not pleased, but she was resigned to me going by this time. "On your own head be it" she told me.

Another War Office letter arrived asking me to attend a Selection Board, again in Bothwell Street. This time there were three officers, no doctors or nurses. The selection board consisted of an officer from each of the services and I was asked which service I wanted to be in. I said the Navy, as I thought that was my best chance of seeing a bit of the world; with a name like 'Nelson' I couldn't be refused. Refused I was; there were no naval vacancies, even for someone with the name 'Nelson'. I thought *what's the sailor doing here if he has nothing to offer?* They offered me the Air Force, but I thought that was liable to land me in Lossiemouth for 2 years, just another bit of Scotland, so I opted for the Army.

Before the end of September a one way train ticket for Aldershot arrived. On my way there I was beginning to feel less confident and a little apprehensive. Scotland and most of England passed outside the train window, giving me plenty of time to wonder if my granny wasn't right in saying I wasn't fit for what lay ahead. At the destination station there awaited an Army lorry and a Corporal with a list of names. My name was shouted and I was herded onto the lorry with lots of other lads of all shapes, sizes and dialects. Most like me were eighteen, but some who had gone to University or finished apprenticeships first, were in their twenties. Awkward and apprehensive, we were let off at Blenheim barracks, the basic training camp for the Royal Army Service Corps. We'd been assigned here according to our civilian jobs – drivers, clerks and firemen. Two other lorries were engaged in discharging their cargo, some guys laughing, others awed and mute. I belonged to the latter category. Half a dozen young white faced Corporals armed with lists, and one bronzed Sergeant, lined us up into groups of twenty, then marched us off, shuffling and out of step (for the last time) to receive uniforms.

Fitting out with uniforms was done by quartermaster privates, in a long, large, unheated Nissen hut. Counters were on the left and a range of cubicles were on the right. These white faced (never been out of Britain) young men, some with plookit faces, sized us up as small, medium, large or extra-large. Thrown down on the counter in front of us were the results of their reckoning. Two of everything; thick serge battledress jackets and trousers, green cotton under clothes, beret and two pairs of boots, one pair for wearing, and as we discovered later, the other for show. We then went into the fitting-out cubicles, to find out if the medium battledress blouse did in fact have medium trousers to match. There was constant coming and going between cubicles and counter, as mediums discovered they were large, and large discovered in Army terms that they were extra-large. Socks were woollen and knee length; I liked them, and kept them for winter use long after my service was finished. Everything not immediately worn was put in a large cotton kit-bag. Civilian clothes were bagged, addressed to home, and sent off later. During all this hustle and bustle Corporals and Sergeants shouted and swore that if we didn't get 'a fucking move on' we were going to get no dinner that night. Under this constant threat we gathered again outside, trying to remember our squads, hardly aided by the shouting and shoving of NCOs. Laggards were shouted at by both NCOs and squaddies already in place and desperate to eat. Nobody wanted to miss their dinner after such a hectic day. All assembled and accounted for, we were marched off to a number of long wooden huts in which were metal bunk beds. At one end there was a large iron wood burning stove, unlighted of course, on this cold October day.

We were introduced to our Corporal in charge, a bespectacled university graduate who was firm, fair and not as foul mouthed as others. He outlined our week ahead, learning to march and to bear arms, but most of all to polish up our boots to a mirror shine 'so that I can see my face in the toe caps'. Then there was the cleaning of the barrack room for the officers' daily inspection. He then marched us to the dining hall to have some food. On return to our bunks we started work on the toecaps of our boots to get that 'mirror shine' that would reflect our Corporal's features. This was not going to be easy; the War Office, for reasons of economy or sadism, had supplied boots in dimpled leather. Before the boots could reflect anything, the dimples had to be smoothed down. This was done with the bowl of a heated tea spoon. Four of us sat round a lit candle, heating our tea spoons, burnishing our toe caps and burning our fingers. This was to go on for several evenings, sweating, swearing and striving for smoothness. It took hours to un-dimple the toe caps, and hours more of spitting and polishing to get the desired mirror effect. Once the latter was achieved, we started on the blancoing of our belts, and the shining up of brass buttons until lights out at 10.30.

The first night was the worst. The baleful un-shaded light bulbs dangling from the ceiling had just gone out, and we'd all fallen into an exhausted dreamless sleep, when suddenly the wretched lights were on again. There was a hideous noise as a Lance Corporal walked the length of the room banging his pace stick off our metal bed frames and shouting "hands off cocks (as if, we were all too tired) hands on socks".

It was 6.30 a.m and dark outside. All we had inside was a horrible cold yellow light from the shade-less bulbs. It was cold, very cold. All over the room guys were struggling out of warm beds, some swearing, some moaning and two crying. As a wee boy with skint knees my grandpa told me 'big boys don't cry'. From the age of six I practiced his advice, and now at eighteen, I'd mastered it. White bodies, some tanned, one or two brown, were getting into unwelcoming Army clothes, cold green cotton underwear, stiff serge trousers, braces, which most of us younger guys had never before suspended trousers from. Only the woollen socks had any warmth of welcome. I and a few others, I could tell, had never been used to cold clothes in the morning. My grandfather had always laid the next day's clothes out over the hot water boiler, so tired bodies on waking were soothed by warm clothes. No such soothing in the Army. My fingers struggled with buttons that had only once before been forced into their button holes. I pulled on my new rough leather boots and laced them up as my grandfather had taught me.

The Corporal poked them with his pace stick. "No cross-lacing in the Army!" he shouted for everyone to hear.

How else do you lace boots? I thought.

The older guy in the next bed showed me how. "Learnt it in the school cadets" he said.

The Corporal wove his way between us, pace stick picking out things not done 'Army fashion' and all the while shouting "Get dressed you lazy bastards! Get a fucking move on! Get washed! Get shaved!" and "Outside on parade in ten minutes, if you want your fucking breakfast!" Some didn't make it, I did. We marched off without the laggards to the cookhouse, for our first Army breakfast. The Army didn't care if you missed your breakfast, or any meal, so long as you were on time for parade.

Breakfast was toast, beans, ham and eggs (not for me). Each item was delivered with a resounding thud onto your plate by the large spoon-wielding Army Catering Corps privates. They tried to knock the plate out of your hands to enjoy your expression as your breakfast slid to the floor. They stood smirking at us novices from behind a long counter covered in large trays of cooling food. Tea was boiled, thick black, with condensed milk and sugar, whether you took either of the latter or not. No choice in the Army. Army meals were a problem for me, with my egg allergy. Not at breakfast as I could see and refuse the eggs there, but lunch and dinner dishes might have eggs in them, so I had to be careful. Being an only child, I never had competition for food and this put me at a disadvantage when treats like jam, marmalade and fruit was put on the table. I was never quick enough to get any as there were gannets on our intake. I didn't starve though and I put on a stone in weight by the end of training. It was all muscle too, due to the route marches, assault course, and combat training.

With breakfast over, we were all marched off to the Regimental Barbers. Berets were removed and so was our hair, by clean sweeps of electric shears over heads and down necks. Some guys, shorn of the lovely long locks they'd been cultivating since puberty, were nearly in tears. We then went out onto the parade ground with our uniformly short bristly heads. It was cold in October without hair, and now our berets were too big. Lining up took some time, with the tallest on the left and short-est on the right. I was about middle. Spacing, right arm up to touch the shoulder of the man to your right, shuffle shuffle, get in line.

Learning to march in step, change step, and keep dis-tance wasn't easy at first. Some guys had great difficulty with all this, and received the stock bawling out from the Corporals, "Were you brought up on a farm, son? No? Then why are you marching like a fucking duck?"

There was no swearing in my grandparents' house, apart from a few 'damns' from my granny, when she had difficulty in threading her darning needle. But I had practiced swearing with my friends, deciding what we were going to do to a particularly disliked bully of a large female teacher we had, in our last year of primary school. So the swearing amused rather than shocked me, unlike some of the lads who had been brought up on a farm and imagined the duck invective was aimed particularly at them.

We were marched round and round the parade ground until we were fairly good at it; not Scots Guards or even Infantry standard, but certainly good novices. Now another challenge was presented to us, having to learn to do it all again with rifles. Lee-Enfields left over from the second world war, to us heavy, weighing about 6 lbs and awkward to handle on parade, with frigid fingers on a cold morning. Sloping arms, presenting arms, grounding arms, and fixing bayonets were all difficult. Rifles were dropped, and there followed the usual diatribe of swearing from the Corporals. "It's not your bird's knickers you're handling, son!"

Then a Sergeant stepped forward and addressed us all. "Drop your fucking rifle on parade and you'd better fall on top of it".

That was it, then; no trying to pick it up, just follow it down in a pretend faint. British soldiers didn't drop their rifles unless they were shot dead in action, or had fainted on parade.

There was one guy in our platoon who was useless on the parade ground. He was a big uncouth farmer's labourer from some remote English county. He couldn't march in step, change step, or turn the correct way when ordered. He was also perennially untidy of uniform, a headache for our Corporal and an embarrassment to the rest of us, who wanted to be smarter than the other lot on parade. Apparently there was usually at least one like this in each platoon. The way the Army dealt with them was to make them permanent 'billet orderlies'. This meant that they kept the billet in good order, cleaned windows, polished the floor and brass-work, all to the required standards of the Corporals or inspecting officers. To us the most important thing was that he lit, and kept alight the iron stove, so that we all had a warm cosy billet to return to after a hard day's square bashing, or worse still, the dreaded assault course. Unfortunately our 'billet orderly' wasn't even good at this. He was regularly taken to task by the team for letting the fire go out, usually on the coldest of days.

By the end of the second week we had our first training with firearms, only .22 rifles to start with, in an indoor range. This was a large low-roofed hanger, with about 25 booths lined up about 20 yards away from a similar number of square card targets, similar to fairground rifle booths. Each target was mounted on a long wire, which could be rolled in to check the accuracy of your shots. If your target came back without a bullet hole in it, you were booked in to spend some of your free time in further practice. It was all very noisy in this large tin shed, so it was difficult to take advantage of the oath-strewn advice of the Sergeants in charge. The smell of cordite was sickening; there were no ear muffs, no health and safety laws then. Ears were ringing and some guys had headaches after this. I managed with a clipped bull, an inner, two outers and a miss, the best of my efforts, to avoid the call back after lunch.

A few days later, after breakfast we were issued with packed lunches and marched to the armoury where we were each given a rifle, and 36 rounds of .303 ammunition. Then we were loaded into Army buses and driven to an outdoor firing range in the countryside around Aldershot. The firing range was a large flat field, with targets at one end and three different firing positions in front of them, at 200, 400 and 600 yards. Behind the targets was a large earth bank, placed there to stop the bullets from going any further. Beside the targets a green flag flew, to be replaced by a red one when firing commenced. The targets themselves were rectangles of linen stretched over metal frames, marked out with concentric circles in black, with a central red bull. Under the targets was an 8ft ditch. This ditch allowed markers, safe from the firing, to mark each individual shot with a long pole ending in a red triangle. A miss was indicated by waggling the pole across the face of the target.

A waggle was usually followed by a loud "for fuck's sake, son; did you leave your white stick in the train coming down here?" The supervising Sergeants were veterans of World War II, and didn't take kindly to National Servicemen. They would move along the lines of the recumbent firers, giving caustic advice in the guise of encouragement. Occasionally a bull would produce a "Bloody good shot, son; you're for the infantry".

Our platoon split, one half going into the markers trenches, the other getting themselves down on the ground in the firing positions according to the requirements of the Sergeants. Before we fired there was the usual "Any questions?" answered rapidly by "No we don't do left handed rifles; this is the Army, not a fucking nursery."

My half of the platoon fired first. Six rounds in your own time, then six rounds rapid fire. The left handers did alright in the 'own time' shoot, but left-handed use of a right-handed bolt seriously handicapped them in the 'rapid shoot'. I settled down, cuddling the butt of the Lee-Enfield to my shoulder and adjusted the magazine of 5 rounds. With one in the breech, that made 6 rounds that we were required to fire off, target and rapid, at each of the three distances. When the red flag appeared beside the targets we started firing.

The Lee-Enfield had a kick like a horse. After my first shot, which nicked the bull, I was loath to press the trigger because of the resultant pain it caused to my shoulder. So I never came near the bull again. Once we'd fired off our twelve shots, we changed places with the markers. There was great massaging of shoulders all round once we were in the ditch.

"Glad you fucking cissies weren't with us on the Western Front" a Sergeant sympathetically exclaimed.

When the rest of our platoon had finished their shoot, we moved on from the 200 yards to the 400 yards mark. This was a more complicated shoot, with wind direction having to be allowed for. This firing practice was not just to teach us to shoot, but to allow the Sergeants to spot potential sharp shooters. There were several of these, farmers' and gamekeepers' sons used to guns, and a few who were just naturally gifted. It followed that these guys would be offered more than the rest of us, higher pay for becoming long-term regulars. Few took this offer up, and those who did generally regretted it.

The 400 yard shoot completed, the Sergeants called for lunch. They gave their voices a rest by switching shouting at us to conversing with each other. Lunch consisted of chicken, beef and egg sandwiches. I swapped my egg ones for chicken or beef. It was a warm day, and the hot sweet tea in the vacuum flasks made me sweat. I held my hot mug of tea to my bruised shoulder for comfort. I thought that this recoil would put any soldier off firing the Lee-Enfield except when the enemy was close at hand and threatening your life. You certainly wouldn't want to pick him off at a distance if he wasn't an immediate danger.

I voiced my concerns about the Lee-Enfield to our Corporal back at the billet that night. He told me the War Office had commissioned a new .280 rifle with little recoil, and was therefore more accurate. When it was ready for service, someone did their maths. They came to the conclusion that the cost of mass-producing the .280 and the ammunition for it made no economical sense, when there were vast stores of .303 ammunition left over from World War II waiting to be used. It was rejected in favour of a new Belgian rifle using .303 ammunition. This semi-automatic was put in service with the Infantry, but not for us National Servicemen. Similarly we had to make do with the World War II mass-produced Sten gun, while the elite units had the new and more accurate Patchet sub-machine gun. The Sten gun fired a lot of rounds very fast, but not very accurately. It fired high to the left, and all my life-size targets were cut diagonally from top to bottom.

One morning, after a couple of hours on the parade ground, we were all marched off to the office block, sat down on uncomfortable metal chairs, and introduced to a sour-faced Scottish Sergeant. He was going to give us a talk on the King's (soon to become the Queen's) Regulations, the Army Bible. Boring us for over an hour, he concluded by asking "Any questions?"

An educated faux innocent voice asked "Is there anything in the King's Regulations that demands an NCO to insert 'FUCK' into every sentence?"

The sour-face became apoplectic. "No there fucking well isn't, and any fucking idiot asking such a fucking idiotic question is liable to find himself fucking out the fucking latrines for the rest of the fucking week!"

There was a stunned silence, then the innocent one began to clap and we all started clapping. Sour-face was not impressed; he looked at his watch and growled "Get the fuck out of my sight". We did and went off to lunch.

Next morning we had bayonet drill. We were all lined up in a row. About fifty yards in front of us and hanging from a wire strung between two gantries was a line of kit-bags stuffed with straw, at body height. We were each handed a bayonet which clipped onto the end of our Lee-Enfields. This bayonet was a big disappointment to me, as it was round and only about a foot long. I'd expected the bayonets I'd seen in paintings of the Argylls in 'the Thin Red Line' at Balaclava, and photos of those of World War I. I expected them to be long like claymores.

"What use are these bloody (I was getting into Army talk) mini bayonets?" I enquired of our good platoon Corporal.

Being a University graduate, he deigned to give me a fuller explanation than I could have expected from any of the other Corporals, who as usual were getting swearing practice in with their men. Apparently the longer bayonets were intended to halt cavalry. No more cavalry, no more long bayonets which were difficult to get out of a corpse, a grave drawback making their users an easy target for the enemy. The shorter bayonet was equally deadly and quicker to use. Noticing that most of our platoon had taken his explanation as an opportunity for resting their tired bodies, our Corporal reverted to normal: "get up, get these bloody bayonets on and get ready for action!"

Action consisted of fixing bayonets, holding the rifles at waist height, howling like a banshee and dashing furiously fifty yards to stick the bayonets into the straw stuffed kit-bags.

The first assault was declared to be useless by the Sergeant in charge. "You are supposed to be frightening these bastards, not greeting them like long-lost fucking friends!"

So we tried to turn up the decibels and charged again. Still not satisfied, the Sergeant swore "Get these smiles off your fucking faces; you're not here to put the bastards at their ease, you're here to kill them!"

So we shouted and screamed obscenities and contorted our faces vilely, all to no avail. We charged and we

LINDLAY NELSON

charged; the kit-bags were now spewing out straw. Our throats were sore, our legs were tired, and we were having difficulty in holding up the rifles. Some were even having difficulty in making the full fifty yards at a run. Still, the remainder of us charged and charged again. For three hours we charged, shouted and obscenely twisted our faces into masks of hate.

The Sergeant's voice was getting hoarser and hoarser. He too had been at it for three hours. Finally he felt it was time to retire to the Sergeants' mess for a beer. "Okay" he shouted. "That's it for now!" Then to groans from some, he added "You bastards who are on your knees, I'll see you lot back here after lunch! Corporal, take their names, have them report to me here at 2 p.m."

There was no afternoon off for us who had survived the morning's bayonet practice. We were all marched back to our billet. Our Corporal told us that there was a monthly competition for the best kept barrack room, and he was in the habit of winning it. So we'd better get down to work, scrubbing the floor, polishing it, cleaning the windows with Brasso, blackening the iron stove at the end of the room. Beds had to be properly aligned, small pack had to be made box shape with the help of cardboard placed inside, placed at the top of the bed with best boots mirror shined, and placed on top. The bedding was to be made neat and tight to hospital standards, with neat corners. All our activity in achieving this exhausted our Corporal, and he had to retire to the Corporals' mess for a beer and a rest. He returned just before dinner to proclaim our efforts

"Not bad, except you need a bit more blackening on the stove".

The next morning before breakfast, and with us all standing to attention by our beds, we were inspected by a spotty faced English private school boy, in a Second Lieutenant's uniform. He walked down between the beds, poked his swagger stick into various corners, uttered a few inanities, and left. Our Corporal looked pleased, but we never knew if we'd won the monthly competition or not. Later we discovered that all the Corporals claimed to be in the habit of winning this competition, if in fact there was such a competition.

It was at the end of the third week when we had returned from a gruelling morning on the assault course, to find our chastened billet orderly had let our fire out again. One of the guys, who'd had a better morning experience than others, helped him re-light it. As we were all milling around drying off our battle fatigue denims, cleaning rifles or lying around exhausted, the barrack room door opened, and a large nasty looking Private blocked the entry.

"You lot outside on parade in 10 minutes" he shouted.

We gaped in amazement. I asked him who he thought he was, a Private giving orders to other Privates. We didn't like it, and our Corporal wouldn't like it.

"Your Corporal's demobbed" he said, with a scowl "and I'm Substantive Private Smith, soon to be Lance

Corporal Smith. I'll be in charge of you lot for the next few weeks".

A groan went up; our good Corporal had gone without warning, and we were getting this 'substantive' (whatever that meant), in his place. I could see that he was not happy with me for being the first to question his authority. I realised that Smith and I were not going to get along; in fact he was not going to get along with anyone.

We lined up outside as asked and were marched by Smith to the administrative block, where we all sat at desks in a classroom. A Second Lieutenant and a Sergeant handed us out papers for an intelligence test, how to cross a river with two planks and three barrels, things like that. I quite enjoyed it, but I could sense from the snorts, shufflings and sighs that some of the others didn't. There then followed a lecture by a Captain on the history of the RASC, during which one or-two unfortunates fell asleep. On waking, they found themselves on latrine duty for the rest of the week. Apparently our Corps had taken over the manning of Royal Artillery guns at Balaclava, their original gunners being dead. This was obviously well beyond the remit of the RASC, and became one of their battle honours. Every afternoon for a week thereafter we were given lessons on the Corps' history, Queen's Regulations and office practice. The following Monday we were given a written exam on all that we had been taught.

The week after we swopped our nice clean warm classroom for a dirty wet cold Monday on the assault course.

We were all exhausted, soaked to the skin and making a hash of everything. Substantive Smith, cosy and dry in his gas cape, was following us around being particularly nasty and abusive. "Get up these ropes quicker, you lazy bastards". "Hold those rifles above the water, you fucking idiots". There were other encouraging pleasantries.

I was having a particularly bad day which started at breakfast. I heard a football commentator drooling on the camp radio as to how on Saturday, at Wembley, England had beaten a 10 man Scotland by a dubious last minute penalty. Things got worse. I dropped my rifle at the water jump and received a sweaty rant from Substantive Smith. I had a particularly tedious rifle cleaning job after dinner that night, so I was in a foul mood when I got back to the billet. I was wet, cold and filthy, and discovered that our billet orderly, seated happily reading the 'Beano', had let the fire go out again.

Unlike some of the others I'd never been particularly nasty to our billet man's shortcomings as a fireman. In this macho environment I think this gave him some idea that I was easy pickings for his humour. He had been addressing me as 'Haggis' for a few days now, and although this annoyed me, I'd let him get away with it in the hope that he'd get tired of his joke and stop it. There was also the fact that he was big and ugly, and I didn't fancy my chances against him. I didn't like it; I didn't see myself as a simile for '...honest sonsy face, Great Chieftain o' the pudding race..', but I hoped that in ignoring it, it would cease. It didn't. However in the midst of morosely removing my soggy wet battle fatigues and propping my filthy rifle against the wall, our billet orderly laid down his comic and smilingly enquired, "'ad a bad day, 'aggis?"

I jumped across the room, gripped him by the throat and testicles, banged him against the wall and said, "Call me THAT ever again and I'll rip your balls off!" I held on tightly to him; his face went purple and I felt fear at having taken on such a big ugly brute.

"Ohhh...just a joke..didn't know it would annoy you".

"It does annoy me!" I responded.

There was a pause. To my great relief he gasped "..nnn..no offence, Jock..Jock alright?"

"Jock's alright" I said, letting him go. A great feeling of relief swept through me. I was not going to be smashed to the floor by this big brute. Deflated I staggered back to bed and collapsed on it. We got on okay after that. Sometimes I even helped him re-light the billet stove, when he'd let it go out, which was often.

A scowling 'Substantive' Smith came in on Monday after lunch to collect us for arms drill. But first he took me aside, his least loved squaddie, and announced that with a Private Goodall from another platoon, I'd come joint first in the IQ tests and exams. All this was said quietly to me, but some of the guys heard it, and joyfully reacted "Swot!" Unlike some others, I had taken notes during lessons and read them over the night before the exam. There were comments of "teacher's pet" and an ironic

"Well done that man there!" This was a phrase used by NCOs to praise some action they approved of, by a Private whose name they couldn't quite remember. There were some genuine remarks of "Well done" from a few.

"Don't let this go to your head" Smith grunted to me, then addressed the platoon "Right, out on parade you fucking lot".

I met Private Goodall with his platoon in the NAAFI a few nights later. His Corporal was buying a round of beers for them all, to celebrate Goodall's success, and the honour that he'd brought to his platoon. Doubtless 'Substantive' Smith, without a NCO's pay, could not afford such a gesture to me and his platoon.

For the next 2 weeks the whole platoon was given typing lessons in the administrative block each morning. They took place in a large room fitted out with individual office desks, on which sat sturdy Imperial typewriters. A Staff Sergeant gave a short lesson on the use of the typewriter. The idea was that we were to be 'touch' typists, something that was unheard of to most of the guys. I was lucky in that I had gone out with one of the girls from the typing pool in the stockbrokers where I worked, and I was used to seeing them type without looking at the keys. This did not help me to master the skill I needed, though. We were all given identical scripts to type from. By the end of the week we were all expected to be able to type a page with only one error. The Staff Sergeant went to the top of the room, and placed a record on a turntable. The theory was that, to get a rhythm going in our typing, we'd do it to music.

The music was interrupted at intervals by 'carriage return' in a loud voice, the idea being that the passage of the music was allied to the time expected for us to type a line of script. It was a bit of a shambles at first. The Staff Sergeant went round the room ensuring that everyone was 'carriage returning' as required. This resulted in some guys returning their carriage with only 3 or 4 words misspelt on the paper. But by the end of the morning most of us were getting the hang of it.

The next morning was a shock. The typewriter keyboards were covered by small table-like appliances, with room for the hands underneath, and the QWERTY keyboard letters on top. We were to learn to touch type looking only at the diagram on top for guidance and not the actual keys. By the end of the first week it was obvious that 'touch typing' was not going to be mastered by most people in the allotted time. On the second Monday morning the Staff Sergeant allowed those who wanted to remove the covers, to type with two fingers if necessary. By the middle of the second week, most of the guys had reached the required standard in this way. Not me; I was determined to master touch typing.

As I didn't seem to be making the desired progress, the Staff Sergeant got more and more annoyed. "Why don't you remove the fucking cover, Nelson? If you're not there by Friday you've failed, and you'll miss your draft to the Middle East and I'll see to it that you're on latrine cleaning for the rest of your service".

I was worried. I didn't want to miss the draft; I didn't want my mates to go off without me. I certainly did not want to spend my service cleaning latrines. The irony of it - top in the exams and the dunce of the typing pool. With idiotic determination, I carried on trying to get my fingers working correctly under the keyboard cover.

Friday 12 noon, sweating profusely, I was the only one left with the Staff Sergeant in the typing room. Noticing he was getting ready to leave, I at last managed to get a touch typed page done to the required standard. The Staff Sergeant grabbed it, gave it a cursory glance, said "Thank fuck", tucked it into his briefcase, and shot out of the room. I'd kept him back from an early lunch in the Sergeants' mess with his mates.

With a great feeling of relief I joined my mates at lunch, not without a bit of mickey-taking from them at my stubbornness. It was water off a duck's back to one who had escaped 'latrine cleaning' at the last minute. After lunch 'Substantive' Bastard Smith, now Lance Corporal Bastard Smith, took me aside; with scarcely concealed scorn, he informed me that my name was on Company Orders to appear before the War Office Selection Board (WOSB) for suitability for officer training. I thought that Smith was having me on, so I went along to the Company Notice Board to look for myself. There was my name, along with Goodall and a couple of others who'd done well in the exams.

An officer? I'd never thought of myself as that. The more I thought about it, the more I liked it. More pay, better food, share of a batman to keep my kit in order, no more itchy uniform. I liked it, and my granny would be proud of me. But best of all, Lance Corporal Bastard

Smith would have to salute me. I particularly liked that bit.

The next week at the appointed time, Goodall, two others and I sat in a small room next to the Commanding Officer's office. I discovered that the other three were private school boys, while I was a public school boy. My alma mater said 'Whitehill Public School' in chiselled letters in red sandstone below the string course of the windows. I never understood the difficulty the English had with discerning the difference between the terms 'Public School' and 'Private School', or their arcane explanations for their belief that 'Private' actually meant Public'. I think they took delight in being different from every other country in the world. The War Office obviously preferred privately educated officers; I had crept in because of my IQ exam excellence and, as I discovered later, our first Corporal's recommendation. The Army needed more officers, and the War Office had decided to offer commissions to National Servicemen in the hope that they'd sign on as regulars. Some did. I'd no intention of doing that, but I definitely fancied being a Sub-Lieutenant, (second class officer) for the rest of my service.

Goodall came out of his interview with a big smile on his face, and gave us all the thumbs up. I was in next. A Major and two Captains sat behind a desk, and to the side of where I sat, was another Captain with a notebook on his knee. The three behind the desk questioned me briskly, while the one to the side took notes, or drew my portrait, whatever. They questioned me firstly on my education, and were clearly impressed when I said I'd been to a public school in Glasgow. There were then questions on Queen's Regulations, Army echelons of power, administration and Corps history. This was the kind of stuff I'd done so well on in the exam, so I was pretty impressive with my answers.

"What would be your attitude to other ranks, i.e. not officers?"

"Oh, I would be respectful and considerate, but firm in my orders". Good answer. I appeared to be doing well, and I was already thinking as an officer.

Then came the question, "You are given a command from a Senior Officer that appears to you to be illegal and immoral. What do you do?"

I felt less confident. I said that it would depend on what were the consequences of following this illegal, immoral order.

They said "Queen's Regulations require you to carry out all orders given by superior officers, and register your complaints later."

"Well" I said, feeling my commission slipping away, "if I'm ordered to shoot prisoners or civilians, complaining about it afterwards is not going to do much good. It's not going to bring them back to life, is it? So I would refuse that order; I wouldn't carry it out".

The three officers looked at each other, nodded to each other, then the Major said, "Thank you, Private Nelson".

As I left I felt disappointed that Lance Corporal Bastard Smith was not going to have to salute me after all, and my granny was not going to have a commissioned officer in her working class family.

It was getting towards Christmas and the New Year. The weather was freezing cold, with snow on the ground - an ideal time for us to spend morning time on the assault course, and long runs to develop stamina. How much stamina did we need as clerks? The afternoon was given over to square bashing, in preparation for our Passing-Out Parade early in the New Year. One night we were all lying around recovering from all of the above, when the Bastard Smith arrived to inform us that the next night we'd be going on a night exercise, something we'd never done before.

Next day we were given the afternoon off, the idea being that we'd sleep so we were fresh for the night exercise. Some slept, some didn't. At 11 p.m. (23 hundred hours in Army speak) we were all marched down, helmeted and in full battle order, to the armoury. We were issued with rifles, Stens and blank (not to be fired within 15 feet of anyone, to prevent cordite burns) ammunition. Then, still yawning and groaning, we returned to our billet, where a Sergeant arrived to brief Bastard Smith as to the purpose and goals of the exercise. He also handed out tins of blackening with which we were to camouflage our white faces. Private Turpin (no relation to the ex-world champion English boxer, but he did look quite like him), asked with a smile if it was necessary for his brown (no PC 'black' then) face to be blacked up.

Somebody shouted "White ointment for Randy!" (nick-named, after the boxer). Randy smiled and gave a two fingered salute to the comedian.

"Everyone blacks fucking up!" ordered the Sergeant.

Smith was given a map and compass, and the co-ordinates of the target. The Sergeant explained to him and us that by lorry we would be taken to the country-side and dumped off. Using the map and compass, we were to navigate our way through a wooded area to find a clearing with a farmhouse. This farmhouse would be defended by another platoon, our enemy for the night. The umpires would consider us successful if we managed to surround the building without losing more than 1/3rd of our men. It was not explained how we would be considered dead by the umpires, assuming that our enemy was also using blank ammunition. Enthusiasm began to replace tiredness; we were begin-ning to think of it as a competition, us against them, a competition that we were determined to win. So we thought, as we were transported off to our destination.

We found ourselves afoot in a large field of snow, lighted by moonlight from a cloudless sky. Using his torch, Smith got our bearings from map and compass. He led us off towards the distant woods. Making our way through the woods was not pleasant. Unseen branches whipped our faces, depositing snow on un-helmeted heads. We were constantly startled by the noise of bats, owls, flapping birds and on the ground, small scurrying animals. We carried on through the trees and shrubbery for about an hour. We were sure that the noise of us, and that of the indigenous inhabitants of the wood, would alert any enemy for miles around. No sign of a clearing, or a farm. The Bastard stopped to check his bearings and then led us on. We became aware that we were recognising some particularly gnarled trees. We were going in circles; Bastard Smith had got us lost.

We had been wandering through this wood for nearly two hours, and were no nearer to our target. We were all hot and tired despite the cold air around us; rifles were getting heavy and hands were freezing on the cold metal of Sten guns. All early enthusiasm to win the day (or night) had gone. We wanted back to a warm billet and bed. Would the Bastard even be able to direct us there? My mate Ray, who had an orienteering badge from the Boy Scouts, was persuaded by us all, reluctantly, to help Smith. We would rather have gone back to billet and beds, but Ray got us to the clearing. An L-shaped farmhouse could be seen, black and darkened except for one lighted window.

A relieved Smith gathered us around him to give whispered instructions. Nasty of personality and useless orienteer as he was, he appeared to have read up on his 'Minor Engagements at Platoon level', (a booklet I knew nothing about until much later in my Army service) and his knowledge here was to restore some faith in him as our leader. We were to surround the building, getting into hidden firing positions, lying in the snow behind the trees, as basic training had taught us. We managed this without, surprisingly, alerting any of the defenders. But only one of us would open fire on the lighted window, our Corporal explained with new found authority, so that all our positions weren't exposed to the enemy. The enemy return fire would give the rest of us targets to aim at, (provided their Corporal hadn't also read 'Minor Engagements...'). We had now regained our initial enthusiasm, and were determined to be adjudged the winners in this combat.

Smith had positioned himself and Randy behind a bush, directly in line with the lighted window. "Fire on the fucking light!" the now exuberant Corporal ordered.

Randy emptied his magazine in the direction of the light. For two long minutes we waited, fingers on the triggers of our weapons, desperate to open fire, but there was no return fire. Suddenly all the lights in the building came on, and a Major with an umpire's yellow sash appeared in the doorway. He ignored the few blanks fired in his direction by trigger-happy over-excited squaddies. Through a loud-hailer he loudly informed us, "THIS EXERCISE FINISHED HALF AN HOUR AGO! You must all return to your point of debarkation, where the vehicles await to take you back to your barracks".

An apoplectic Lance Corporal Bastard Smith had to be helped to his feet by Randy. The rest of us rose, wiping the snow from our now damp uniforms and cursing to each other about our incompetent Bastard Corporal. Said Corporal, bitterly disappointed by his own ineffi-ciency in orienteering, meekly let Ray lead the traipse back through the dark woods to the awaiting transport. This became more difficult as cloud now obscured the moonlight.

By this time our 'haggis' man was getting the hang of keeping the stove going until we came in of a late afternoon, chilled to the bone. The stove would then be opened up to a hearty blaze. The trouble was that a 'hearty blaze' didn't last long, on the Quartermaster's allocation of one pail of firewood and coal per day. We needed extra supplies. There were none. The Quartermaster's coal shed was guarded night and day by fire pickets armed with pick handles. They could be bribed, but would only give 2 large lumps of coal for 10 Woodbine, and our smokers were unwilling to donate too many of their fags to the cause. We went out in parties to hunt for anything combustible to make our evenings comfortable, but all the other platoons were on the same search. Two platoon huts each shared a bath house. Some vandal had the idea of breaking up the wooden bath boards for fuel. Then it was the benches that we sat on to dry ourselves. The two platoons co-operated in stripping the bath house of everything combustible. It was necessary to do this with care, not to alert the camp authorities. Wood had to be split into lengths able to fit down the legs of trousers. Stiff legged soldiers would cross in ant like files, from bath house to barracks, saluting with unusual care any passing officers. LC Bastard Smith turned a blind eye to all this; he might not like us, but he liked to reside in our warm barrack room.

The Army had devised a system for Christmas and New Year's leave. 48 hour passes were given for one or the other. Scotsmen held the fort at Christmas, the English, Welsh and Irish at New Year. 48 hours was of no use if you came from Glasgow or Wick, or Newcastle or Carlisle for that matter, so real benefit only went to those within a few hours journey from Aldershot. Furthermore, there was a ratio of 9 Anglos to 1 Scot. Some of the English were annoyed that so many of them were held back at New Year, to allow a few Scots to go out on the town. Some of the Northern Anglos joined the Scots in taking the New Year pass.

My mates, Ron and Ray, being from Newcastle, had the same home-going problems as myself. They decided to take the New Year pass, and on Hogmanay we went into Aldershot town centre together. We visited a few pubs, bought a half bottle of Johnnie Walker, and after a fish supper we decided to try our luck at the local dance hall. Of luck there was none. The local girls found the local boys preferable to us gauche youths with shorn hair, prickly uniforms and smelling of booze. All the girls I fancied refused to dance with me. Then there was a 'woman's choice' and a nice wee round fat plain girl, in a hideously flowered dirndl skirt asked me to dance. I felt obliged to give her a few more dances as the night wore on, but I couldn't bring myself to walk her home. Ron, Ray and me saw in the New Year down in the toilets, finishing off our bottle of whisky, as the band above played 'Auld Lang Syne'. We then staggered, singing raucously, back to our billet, where we woke the sleeping Londoners with fond off-key renderings of 'Scots Wha Hae' and the 'Bladen Races', and noisy non-reciprocated wishes of a 'Happy New Year'. The next evening, when our heads had cleared, we went to the cinema, as we couldn't face another night dancing.

Festivities past, we all now concentrated on preparing for our Passing Out Parade. Uniforms cleaned and pressed, small pack squared and placed with best boots on top, situated at the head of the bed, with all sheets pulled flat and tight and tucked in neatly at the corners. Windows were cleaned with Brasso, as were the metal fittings. The floor was scrubbed, dried and polished to a high shine, all done under the baleful eye of Lance Corporal Bastard Smith. He did not want his first month as an NCO to be blemished by a black mark given to him, as a result of the indolence of his platoon. Primary inspection would be by our platoon Sub-Lieutenant; if we were lucky or unlucky, depending on the outcome, we might get a visit from the inspecting General. Haggis man was left in the billet, to keep everything shining, to see no beetles scurried across our pristine floor, to see no spiders spun on our windows, and hopefully to keep the stove going to warm our return.

Parents, relatives and girlfriends were invited to the Passing Out Parade. As usual it was only those living within a reasonable distance from Aldershot, or very rich enthusiastic Army people, who bothered to turn up. The parade went well. We kept in line, we kept in step, and we kept our 'eyes right' on passing the General (Lieutenant General, whose name I've forgotten), and we kept our urine in our bladders. We'd been on the parade ground for over 2 hours, on a bitterly cold day. The camp inspection went well, too; the General did inspect our billet, and seemed pleased, much to Bastard Smith's relief. We later heard that the Quartermaster suffered the General's wrath for not having provided suitable bath boards and benches in the bath house. We all feared later retaliation from the Quartermaster Quarter.

Now that we were accredited soldiers issued with War Office flashes to sew on our battle blouses, we were given 2 weeks pre-embarkation leave. A pre-dated return train ticket to Glasgow was provided, so off I went in neatly pressed uniform and polished boots to see my grandparents and my father if I was lucky, and he didn't have something more pressing to do. My girlfriend Ina, whom in a moment of enthusiastic amour 3 months after my 17th birthday, I'd made my fiancée, was on the Central Station platform to greet me. I intended to spend a lot of time with her in the next fortnight. Of course I got a warm welcome from my grandparents; my grandfather handed me a bottle of whisky, which apparently I'd won with a raffle ticket bought the night before I'd left for Aldershot. He hadn't drunk it, as some of my pals' fathers would have done. My granny gave me a warm welcome, with no apparent annoyance at my bad behaviour before I left. But her rheumatics were bad, and she needed help to rise from her chair, and now walked with a stick. I was glad she didn't have that before I left, or I might have got it over my shoulders for my annoyance at her doing what she thought was best for me.

I enjoyed being back in Glasgow and in comfortable civilian clothes again. I suppose that all soldiers on leave get a certain amount of attention from family and friends; they know you are not going to be with them for very long, and they treat you as a refugee from a strict regime that they know little about. But I never really felt that I was a soldier; it was like I was in a bit of theatre, a long running play in which I had a role as a soldier. In the pub with pals, who for one reason or another were not in the services, one was treated with a certain amount of respect as the one who was fitter than them, and was able to take Army training. With all my absences at school due to my asthma, this was a new experience for me. I enjoyed it. I also enjoyed being back with home-made cooking, not having to wonder if a dish had eggs in it. My fiancée worried me though, with her desire that I accompany her to the church. My 14 days away from Aldershot were too precious to be wasted on religion. I had met Ina at the Riddrie Scottish Episcopalian Church. This Church claimed to be the pre-Reformation Church of Scotland. My pals and I from the age of 16 formed its choir, mainly so we could avail ourselves, after service on a Sunday, of the Church Hall snooker table. I wasn't religious. The Church of Scotland, to which I had been taken as a child, had never convinced me of its message. When I met Ina I was 17 and she was a nice-looking 21. There was nothing more exciting to a teenage male than to have a good looking older woman fancy you. I was hooked.

Leave over, I returned to Aldershot. Everything was now geared to our leaving for the Middle East, or Egypt, as we were told at the last minute. Injections were needed to protect us against diseases that were unknown in Britain. So one surprisingly sultry after-noon in February, the whole draft lined up to enter a small wooden cabin. Through the open door we could see medical staff lined up left and right at rows of small tables, with all sorts of syringes and sticking plasters lying about. We could see that we were to file between the medics with our arms bare; we would then have 2 jabs in one arm, and 3 in the other. The end medic would then apply sticking plasters to the wounds. There was a heavy smell of antiseptic emanating from the hut. It was slightly sickening, and a few soldiers were overcome by it and the sight of the awaiting needles; they swooned away even before entering the hut. I was pleased to note that one or two of them were from the crack regiments of the British Army, the Paras and Commandoes. There were some Womens' Royal Army Corps in the queue, but they were alright, and some went to the aid of the recumbent soldiers, helping them to the back of the queue.

Chapter 2

HAGGIS IN THE DESERT

At last we were on our way out to Egypt, seated in a chartered Hermes airliner, with sexy air hostesses who had long nylon-covered legs and tight bums. We were not to see the like again for 19 months. We were treated like royalty and had our human dignity back; most of us young men had never had such a luxurious indolent experience before. We had lunch and afternoon tea on a tray in our laps, with crisps, nuts and sweets on demand from the aisle trolley. We even had a can of beer and all of it was free. For me, my first air flight was a fabulous new experience; we flew through the thick cloud, out of the rain below, into clear blue skies to infinity. I loved it. This part of the Army experience was great; Lance Corporal Bastard Smith was left behind to be nasty to the next intake. We were human beings again. We were heading for sunny Egypt, the pyramids and all that. It was exciting, but on the long haul some guys fell asleep. Not me, I was far too excited by all this novelty.

Hours later the pilot announced on the intercom "Egypt". What a disappointment. We were flying down through thick dark clouds such as we'd left in the south of England. Sunny it wasn't, and there was not a pyramid in sight. But there was no rain as we got off the plane, and it was warm for February. In fact we were not to see rain again for another 15 months. An Air Force Sergeant, polite by Army standards, lined us up on the tarmac, while another supervised the unloading of our packs and kitbags from the hold of the plane. We were then marched off, sweating profusely in our serge battle dress uniforms, packs on backs, kitbags on shoulders, to a long transit hut at the far edge of the airfield. We were white, everyone else was tanned. There were some sandbagged machine gun posts at points around the airfield. From them some RAF Regiment guys, tanned and cool looking in their blue uniforms, laughed at us and shouted "Hey, Pinkos! You Sprogs!" But we'd been battle hardened by our basic training back in Aldershot, and some shouted back in true Army NCO speak "Fuck off, you toy soldiers!"

But 'Pinkos' was to be the generic name for us all until we got a tan, and 'Sprogs' until that tan allowed us to merge with our longer serving mates. That night some of us didn't sleep well in our Nissen hut. The excitement of the day had been too much; it was hot and stuffy, the beds were hard, and there was the loud snoring of those unaffected by any of the former.

In the morning we were loaded into sand coloured lorries, and driven at high speed along the Suez Canal road, to our camp in Moascar Garrison Village. We were escorted by armed soldiers in sand coloured Land Rovers, with long metal angle irons rising to above roof height from their front bumpers. Later we learnt that these were there to protect the drivers and occupants from decapitation. In order to maximise air flow in the Egyptian heat, drivers would lower their front windows, leaving them in danger from wire strung across the tree lined road by terrorists. These trees were there to provide very necessary shade but they now also meant danger. So this was our introduction to active service and danger. This was what we were being paid an extra 6p a day for, putting our lives in danger to keep the Suez Canal British.

Moascar was a Garrison town built by the Army after the British had taken over the Canal from the French. It was a few miles to the west of the Egyptian town of Ismailiya, which was at the entrance to the Canal. Moascar was built to guard the Mediterranean entrance to the Canal. It was constructed by the Victorians, pushing the desert back a few miles. In times of danger, we filled sand bags with this desert, and brought it back into Moascar. Looked at from the air, it had the shape of a tadpole. The head of the tadpole consisted of a circle of red sandstone barracks of two storeys with balconies, surrounding a parade ground. There was an outer circle of separate apartments, married quarters for regular officers and NCOs, a stone built mansion with walled garden, for the General Officer Commanding HQ BTE (Headquarters British Troops in Egypt) and two large wooden huts for the General's staff called `G Branch'. This was where my mates and I would work. From the head of this tadpole stretched a tail, pretentiously called 'The Mall'. It was a road about a mile long; on either side was the main tented accommodation for the infantry regiment guarding the town. There were also a few shops let out to local businesses, barbers, tailors where you could have your uniform customised to your own liking, and laundry, pressing and dry cleaning facilities, known as the 'dhobi wallahs'. There was also a walled open air cinema, and a Command Library. For anything else one had to travel to Fayid, or less likely, due to lack of security, Ismailiya. Moascar was completely surrounded by a high security fence with guard towers at strategic points. This was to be our home for the next 19 months.

We were pleased with our quarters in Moascar. They were on the top floor of one of the red sandstone buildings solidly built by the Victorians. The red sandstone reminded me of Glasgow tenements of the same period. We were very lucky to be in stone buildings; the infantry men were in tents, unbearably hot in the summer, and prey to scorpions, other ground bugs and mosquitoes. Bed bugs and mosquitoes were our main annoyances. The bed bugs bred in cracks in the stone walls, entered our beds when we were absent, waited in the corners of the metal frames to come out at night and bite us on our backs and bums. Full of our blood, they were like swollen red peas, and too fat to scurry back to their lairs in the stone walls. The morning after being bitten, we'd dump our metal beds on the stone floor, the bugs would fall out, and we'd crush them with our heavily studded boots. Mosquitoes were a different problem. They came out at night after dinner, when we exchanged shorts for trousers and wore scarves to protect against bites. Canal Zone mosquitoes were not malarial, but they gave you a nasty bite that turned into a sore lump the next day, and lasted for about a week. We were provided with heavy green mosquito nets which we were supposed to sleep under each night. Unfortunately in the hot summer nights they cut out any breath of air that was available, so we only tended to use them when we heard the 'zizz' of a mozzy in the room.

Everyone let their nets down then. The worry was when the 'zizz' had stopped, which meant the mozzy had landed on its target. On occasions when a mozzy was trapped inside a net, there would be cursing and swearing and a bed overturned noisily, as its inhabitant jumped out enmeshed in his mosquito net, and tried to swat the unseen enemy. There would be cheers from those still awake, and oaths from those awakened from their sleep. No sympathy was ever offered.

I was one of the first into the toilets on our first morning in Moascar barracks. I had learned back in Aldershot of the importance of this, in order to ensure hot water and a basin for oneself to shave in. The wash room consisted of half a dozen ancient basins with cracked mirrors above, all down one side of a long room with a tiled floor. Along the opposite wall was the same number of WC's. Of hot water that morning there was none, and often in the future months there wouldn't even be cold water. Stripped to the waist I started to shave. Suddenly I was startled by a loud noise behind me. I turned and saw a long thin Arab with a wrinkled dark face, in a djeballa, a sort of daytime nightshirt, mopping away at the floor. This was my first encounter with an Egyptian. I felt nervous but managed a "Good morning". He grinned at me with teeth stained, (I learned later) by betel juice, said something indistinguishable to me, then turned his back and carried on mopping. I suddenly felt all alone in a strange land, in a place I didn't want to be, and not at all a brave soldier lad. Then all at once I felt better. In rinsing my shaving brush I noticed the sinks bore the label, 'Shanks of Barrhead'. So here I was sleeping in a barracks built in Glasgow tenement red sandstone, and equipped with genuine Glasgow sinks. I almost felt at home. I went whistling cheerily back into the room where some of my mates were moodily easing themselves out of their beds to face the dawn of their second day in Egypt.

After making up beds and squaring off kit to sit on the bed head, we breakfasted and then fell in on the parade ground outside our barracks. There a Pay Corporal Sergeant read out a list of our postings within the camp. My mates and me, having done well in the IQ tests and exams, were despatched to 'G' (standing for General's) Branch, where we would be clerking for the General Staff of Lieutenant General Sir Francis Festing, Commander in Chief of HQ BTE (Headquarters British Troops in Egypt). We were in `G' Operations, and had to sign the 'Official Secrets Act', which prevented us talking about our work there for the next 20 years. In charge of the Branch was a World War II veteran, an SSM, (same as RSM, only Staff Sergeant Major). While RSMs were preferred tall, and of a commanding disposition, such was not the case for SSMs. Ours was of average height and sallow skinned. He did not have a great sense of humour but did have a great sense of responsibility and respect for Queen's Regulations. He had a number of scary stories of his experiences during World War II that he liked to relate to us. We didn't come in contact with too many soldiers who'd been in the war, so we were eager to listen to one who had been.

We were given desks and typewriters and a brief outline of what was expected of us. We would be on duty from 7 a.m. until 1 p.m. in winter, and 6.30 a.m. until 12.30 p.m. in the heat of summer. We were to type out Operational Orders, training schedules and Intelligence Reports for the Canal Zone originated by the General and his Staff Officers. These would be distributed to the concerned regiments throughout the Zone, by the Signal Message centre, sited within our Branch. There would also be copies of all this material to go to the General's House, outside working hours. For the purposes of this, a World War 1 bicycle was provided. It was then discovered that a private hailing from Cornwall, who could drive a tractor on his father's farm from the age of 10, couldn't ride a bicycle. Two of us were 'volunteered' to teach him with immediate effect.

In addition to all this we would be put on a rota for Branch Night Duty. As signals came into the Signal Message centre throughout the night, two men were required to spend the night there processing them. From time to time during the night the 'G' Branch Duty Officer would call in to inspect any signals received, and give orders as to what action was to be taken if need be. This might include a night time bicycle ride from the Branch to the General's house, about ¼ mile away. We were provided with a camp bed so that we could have turns each at a short sleep during the night. The idea was that there was always someone awake the whole night. On quiet nights it was easy for both men to fall asleep. This was a chargeable offence. The Branch, for security reasons, had to be locked from the inside all night, so if the Duty Officer called and couldn't get in - and he was a stickler for the rules - then a charge would be laid. Most of 'G' Branch officers valued the good relations they had with their clerks, however, and would give them a little leeway. All we got for our 24 hour vigil was the next day off, and excused camp guard room duties, except in an emergency.

"When will the summer come?" I asked the SSM.

"April" he said. "Enjoy the winter; the summer will be long, hot and sweaty".

"I'm sweating now" I said.

"Not like you will in April" was the reply.

I thought *summer in April, just in time for my birthday.*

As clerks we didn't have much to do in the way of marching. Entering the Pay Office every month, marching up to the Pay Corps Officer's desk, was about it. Coming smartly to attention with the right boot thumped down on the floor "Pay and pay book correct, sir", salute, smart turn and march back towards the door, where a Corporal or Sergeant stationed there would probably bark "haircut, soldier". We did notice when lining up in front of the Pay Office, that the trousers of those who had longer service than us were hanging better and had straighter seams than ours. The bottoms hung neatly over their gaiters, whereas ours stuck up untidily. To rectify this we needed 'trouser weights'. These weights would be worn inside the trouser leg, where the bottom was tucked inside the gaiters. There they held the trousers tightly over the gaiters, and kept the ironed crease nice and straight throughout the day. Ronnie Ross and I decided we needed to get a set of weights.

I swapped two pieces of cord for two metal lavatory chains. They weren't heavy enough for our purposes. Ron and I needed some rings of lead to be added. Where to get it? The roof was the answer. We'd learnt from those about to be demobbed that it never rained in Moascar, so the roof really didn't need its lead. So late one night Ronnie and I climbed onto the roof and onto the lead gutter which separated the Sergeant's room from our barrack room. It hadn't occurred to us that the camp searchlights not only swept the perimeter of the camp, but also the rooftops. We had to dodge their glare as we cut away with our Stanley knives; we didn't want to be shot as terrorists. We got down safely eventually, with enough lead to make ourselves probably the best set of weights of all the camp 'pinkos'.

April came and so did the sun. I went to bed; it was hot and the night sky was overcast. I awoke to a clear blue sky and a hot yellow rising sun. Those, to whom this was a second summer, assured us that this was the weather now until November. And so it proved. Born in a land which could have all the seasons in one day, this was a revelation. Weather, as such, did not exist in Egypt during the summer; it was just clear blue sky, sun and heat without variation. The meteo forecast consisted of an estimate of the temperature, usually somewhere between 90 - 120 degrees Fahrenheit, (no Celsus in those days for the British Army). Asthma I no longer had. The very hot dry weather and a minimum of green vegetation seemed to suit my lungs. We packed away our serge uniforms and were issued with khaki drill, shorts, shirts and puttees that were wrapped around your legs above boots, to keep the sand out. These uniforms had to be washed and starched every two or three days. This was a job that the local Arab camp laundry did for a few ackers (about 6p); they were known as the 'dhobi wallahs'.

After finishing duty at noon, the afternoon was an exhaustive lying about on bed reading, writing home, playing cards or sleeping. Sometimes we'd make a journey down to the NAAFI for a cool beer and play the duke box. Other times at night when it got cooler, we'd check out at the Guard House, a security arrangement, to ensure that you were back in time and fit for duty the next day, and walk down the 'Mall', visit the open air cinema, or sit in the local café drinking. Opening of the cinema was irregular; it was an event when there was a show on, and nearly everyone attended. Films were well advertised in advance. Unlike Britain, there was no censorship. We saw some good films there, the uncut 'Wild Ones' with Marlon Brando, and the newly released (1953) 'Mr Hulot's Holiday' with Jacques Tati. For us it was a strange experience, sitting in an open air cinema on a hot night, the film on the screen shot across from time to time by night insects, moths and mosquitoes, and hearing the chirping of the crickets and croaking of the bullfrogs when the screen was silent. Arabs in the employment of the Army were allowed in, and for their benefit there were two side screens of sub-titles in different Arabic languages. This just added to the exotica of the open air cinema experience for us.

The wooden huts of 'G' Branch where we worked became unbearably hot towards noon and lunch time, despite the whirling fans on ceiling and desk. With the heat, tempers during this period began to get a little frayed. The SSM became more irascible than usual. The main victim of this was our Cornishman, whose sole skill seemed to be in tractor driving, not something in great demand in 'G' Branch HQ BTE. We had sympathy for his plight. Obviously he was bright enough; he had a very polite voice for a farmer's lad, and he'd done well in the exams, or he wouldn't have been with us. A phrase I learnt later probably summed him up 'Clever, with no common sense'. Sympathy for him diminished when we had to re-do his work which didn't come up to the SSM's requirements. The latter began to give him the more menial tasks to do. Due to our continual perspiration in the heat, it was necessary to have regular liquid intake. This consisted in the main of hot sweet tea, delivered in shiny metal pails from the cook-house. The delivery was made by an inmate of the Guard House serving sentence for some folly, sandwiched between two Regimental Policemen (RPs), marching him at a Light Infantry pace. This was not a pleasant experience for someone trying not to spill anything from a heavy pail of tea on each arm. Once the pail was delivered to us, it became the Cornishman's duty to share it out in chipped mugs to us all. SSM was first, with an unchipped mug, of course, NCOs next then us privates. It was very sweet tea by the time we got it. The duty cook would just empty a box of sugar and a can of condensed milk into the tea in the pail, leaving the swinging delivery of the man on 'jankers' to mix it. The milk mixed well, the sugar not so well. Everyone took milk and sugar in their tea; no choice, that was the Army way. Once back in civilian life, I never took tea with milk and sugar again.

On Branch duty one afternoon, I had to leave the Cornishman in control while I delivered by bicycle an urgent message to the General's house. The former had not yet mastered keeping upright on two wheels for a sufficient length of time to reach the General's mansion. I creaked to the gate on the old rusty bike, and was waved in by the guards. To my surprise the General was in his vegetable garden digging away, while his wife gave orders from the pathway. The General, a tall, hearty, bulky man, was sweating profusely, surprisingly dressed in an olive green Army issue singlet, shorts, socks and boots, all as issued to 'other ranks'. On his head was a battle dress forage cap. There was also a hole in his singlet. Compared to his wife in her floral frock and large straw sun hat, he looked like a well-fed tramp. He was later to become Chief of the Imperial General Staff. He read the message and was joined by his ADC (Aide de Camp), who took the message and went off to deal with it. The General called him back, pointed at the bike and said, "get their Colonel to put in a requisition for a new one".

On duty General Festing's preferred uniform was strictly non-regulation, jodhpurs and calf-length leather boots.

Neither did his attitude to personal security concur with that of the Provost Marshal. He caused concern to his Military Police escorts, by driving himself at great speed to the units under his command. The Provost Marshal provided MPs in two angle iron Land Rovers, with Bren machine guns mounted, to sandwich the General's Staff car on visits outside the camp. Festing would commandeer the lead Land Rover and drive it himself at a pace that the driver of the empty Staff car, and the MPs in the other Land Rover, had difficulty keeping up with. On reaching his destination, the General, exhilarated, face red with sun and the buffeting of the hot wind, would hand the driver's keys back to his driver, turn to his ADC and say "good as an early morning brisk walk, that, what?". So we were told by our SSM, who knew the Provost Marshal, to whom the MPs in question often complained of the General's disregard for his own, and their safety.

At this time in the Branch we were all appointed as sort of secretary typists to the officers commanding the various arms of 'G' Branch. That's to say 'G' Operations, 'G' Intelligence and 'G' Training. I was working for a very nice Captain Scott of 'G' Training, a slim fit Englishman with a lot of energy, and a fine ginger moustache. It reminded me of the one worn by my grand uncle Jock (real name, not generic) Buchanan, who had been an RSM in the Royal Scots Fusiliers. He walked very straight backed, up Balfron main street with his collie dog, twirling his waxed moustache as he went. Captain Scott would do the same twirling, head bent over a typing draft. 'G' Training had the largest output of bumph, everything from rifle cleaning, to equipping tanks and armour for a desert assault. The theory of the use, maintenance and supply, of armour and infantry with support aircraft in the different theatres and terrains of war, was the subject of promotional exams for officers. The War Office sent out the exam papers, and Captain Scott provided a list of officers in varying units in the Middle East who were to take the exams. It was my job to type and post the letters to the units concerned. Scott was energetic and efficient, and he was happy with my work. He put me up for promotion to Lance Corporal, but nothing came of it. I thought that the SSM, who had probably read my Officer Selection Board report, decided that I did not have the proper respect for Army authority. Unfortunately Captain Scott was promoted to Major and was posted back to his regiment.

My new officer was an acting Major from the New Zealand Army Staff Corps. He looked and spoke like a colonial James Mason. He was a very nice guy, this Major Malcolm, but a bit dim, lacking the energy and drive of Captain Scott. However I liked him, and we got on well together, though on one occasion I let him down badly, and on another I saved his bacon. The Major had submitted a brief to our Colonel in charge of 'G' Branch, on the standing down of a Carrier Pigeon Unit that was no longer required after its use in World War II. I had typed, from his draft, for the presentation. The next morning at 'Colonel's prayers' (the staff meeting of officers reviewing the operational requirements for the day), the Colonel had taken the Major to task for spelling 'pigeon', as 'pidgeon'. Of course I'd copied it from his draft, without noticing the error. I then seemed to have some sort of brain impediment, despite the fact he showed me a dictionary spelling of the word. I maintained that it could also be spelt `pidgeon'. After all, I'd kept racing pigeons as a young teenager, so I should know about their spelling. I proposed to write home to my grandfather and ask him to send me out one of my pigeon year books as proof. The Major was profoundly relieved by my assurance, and the fact that he would be able to put the Colonel right on the matter, thus restoring some literary credence amongst his fellow officers, who had been teasing him about the error. Of course, when the Racing Pigeon Annual arrived, I discovered to my horror that there was no alternative spelling of 'pigeon'. Luckily some time had elapsed between the original error, and my Pigeon Annual arriving. The Major had almost forgotten the matter, didn't take my squirming apologies too badly, and asked me to baby-sit for him the next evening.

Baby-sitting for regular officers and NCOs who had their families in married quarters, was one of the perks for us National Servicemen. Husbands and wives would go out to mess parties, or to dinner in each other's homes, and they would require not just a baby-sitter, but a guard for their children in their absence. This was for us a great break from sitting reading, writing home, playing cards, listening to the radio, or just sleeping the evenings away in our billet. Baby-sitting gave you a night with a well stocked fridge, lots of beers and comfortable chairs and sofas to relax in, while listening to a radio with better sound, and stations that you could actually choose, rather than the received ones of our billet's radio. Major Malcolm had a nice garden full of scented flowers and exotic palms. Sitting in it, of a star glittering hot night, listening to the crickets chirping and the bull-frogs croaking, taking in the sweet smells and warmth of a tree shaded garden, was balm to the soul of the soldier uprooted from his home comforts.

As befits somebody who looked like James Mason, the Major had a very handsome looking wife, tall with a pert mischievous face. She was very elegant, slim, and dressed in a long flowing gown in grey, looking much like a Whistler 'Harmony in Grey and White'. She was something that my mates and I had not seen the like of since entering the Army. She was charmingly polite to us all, in a way that no British Army officer's wife, too aware of her status, was. Deprived of female company for so long, we all loved, or lusted, or both, after her. There were a few female soldiers, Womens Royal Army Corps, WRACS, in the camp, but none of them had any time for other ranks, not when there were high ranking NCOs and junior officers able to entertain them in the club-like atmosphere of Sergeants' and officers' messes. All we privates could offer women was the NAAFI, an area of male drinking, bonding and sometimes punch-ups. Any female that you would want to have, would not want to go there with you. The alternative was a walk arm-in-arm around the camp, in and out of the palm-lined paths between the huts. But women were only available on a few occasions to sight, and not to touch. Sometimes not to appreciate, either. One hot afternoon (weren't they all) a young and pretty Sergeant called at our Branch to collect some mail for her com-manding officer. As she walked off down the path from our hut one of our Lance Corporals gave her a wolf whistle. She waggled her hips in appreciation. Next minute there appeared in the doorway of our hut, out of nowhere, a Captain raised from the ranks of some obscure English county regiment. His ugly face red with apoplectic rage, he demanded to know who had broken Queen's Regulations by making inappropriate wolf whistles at a female NCO. None of us, including our SSM, had heard or seen anything contravening said Regulations, so we had to stand listening to a harangue on the duties of respect for Army rank and the female sex. When he had gone off back to his den, we then had to listen to our SSM telling us of the dire things he would do to us if, in his Branch, anything like this were ever to happen again.

Shortly after this I underwent an even greater humiliation than the episode with the spelling of Major Malcom's 'pigeon'. With winter approaching (a relative concept this, with temperatures descending to 85-75F and still sunny) the Branch decided to get a football team together, to play other branches and camps in the area. They couldn't find a goalkeeper, so I foolishly volunteered. Because in my youth running about brought on my asthma, I'd always played in goal, and played there in many floor football games with the Boy Scouts. I had good hand to eye co-ordination and I was quick, so I had become a good keeper at that level. So on a hot sunny afternoon the 'G' Branch team trotted out in Army boots, woollen socks and olive green Army vests, onto the nearby sandy football pitch. We were faced with the 16th Independent Parachute Brigade Group team, in Queen's Park jerseys, shorts and football boots. Who was the silly bastard that had decided that our inaugural game should be against the Paras?

From the kick off it was obvious that we didn't have a defence. All our guys were up ineffectually trying to knock in goals at the other end. Our rugby linesman of a referee didn't seem to know anything about the offside rule. The Paras wee right winger had a free run down the wing, and I could see their goliath of a centre forward bearing down on me. The winger put in a high cross and I moved smartly off the goal line to collect it before it reached the centre's head. I caught and held it well. Then I woke up, with the sun and several team mates looking anxiously down on me, and the referee trying to separate their centre and one of our larger team members. It was pointed out to the referee that this was a free kick and sending off offence. We got the free kick. Shaken, and with a bit of double vision, I skied it into the path of their goliath, who rammed it into the net. Not being too clear about what I was seeing, having a large bump coming up over one eye, and a left arm grated red by sand, I let in another 5 goals before the interval. I was replaced in goal for the second half. Now as a half back, I tried to get revenge on their wee winger, but he was too good and too fast for me, and their centre was too big. My humiliation was complete, so was that of the team; we lost 10-0. The team supported me, but for several days I had to stand jibes from our touchline supporters. The worst were from fellow Scots, who felt I'd let down Scottish football.

One afternoon a week an escorted bus made its way from our camp to Lake Timsah beach. We all piled in. A day on the beach, in and out of the water, was not only an escape from the afternoon heat of our billet and its surrounds, but a chance for us new arrivals to become less 'pinko'. A portion of the beach had been reserved behind high barbed wire fencing for the use of the British Forces. It was guarded and patrolled by one of the infantry regiments. However, local trusted trades people were allowed in under licence to sell ices, hamburgers and other delicacies. These were a treat for us, more succulent and varied than anything available at the NAAFI. There was always a Turkish strong man at the gate who, as well as lifting heavy weights, would stick hat pins through his jaw. A fire eater blew flames into the air, and various small boys offered porn and their sisters: "hi McGregor (the HLI from Tel el Kabir, were on guard here) you like my sister, only 13 and never been kissed. Only 10 ackers." Our Army pay may have been low, but by Egyptian standards we were rich. There was always an acker or two for the strong man and his mate, and for one acker (sixpence, if I remember correctly) I bought an unopened copy of 'Lady Chatterley's Lover'. I knew nothing about D.H. Lawrence; I just thought that reading this thick book would pass the afternoons pleasantly back at the billet. It did, once I had sliced the pages open. I later learnt from an Education Corps Corporal that this was a traditional French book binding. Once I'd read it, it went round the room, though to some, only a few pages were of interest.

One problem I had on the beach was that I couldn't swim, despite having been in the school with the best swimming and life saving record in Scotland. The chlorinated water of the school's indoor pool brought on my asthma. Lake Timsah's water was heavily salted, and it was easy to swim and float there. The water was warm, and some undercurrents were quite hot. But I couldn't swim, so I played around in the water with my pals, got hot, came out onto the sand, which was too hot for my feet, laid down on my towel to sunbathe and fell asleep.

I was awakened by my mate Ray saying "I think you've had enough." I was no longer pink, I was scarlet all over. I felt shivery, in 110 degrees? I had sunburn. Once dressed, my starched uniform shorts cut like a knife into my thighs. My hard pay-book in my left hand khaki drill jacket pocket, grated on my left chest, but it had to be kept there, Army orders. Back at the billet I sat on my bed and peeled a square foot of skin off my thigh. I was sick, but fascinated by this piece of skin, with all its tiny hair holes.

Somebody said, "the Nazis would have made a lamp-shade out of that". A Corporal gave me a tin of Nivea cream to rub on myself. I couldn't do it; it was too sore, too cold on my fevered skin. I couldn't go sick, I'd have been put on a charge for rendering myself unfit for duty. It took me about ten days of agony in bed, out of bed and at work to get over it. When all the burnt skin had peeled off, I was 'pinko' again.

About a month later I was in the NAAFI, idly looking at the camp information board, covered in the 'Dear John' letters that some of the guys had received from their unfaithful girlfriends. I noticed a small advert there for a 'Course of Confirmation in the Church of England'. I had no idea what this meant, but what attracted me was that it took place over a week at Lake Timsah. I could see myself having a very relaxed week at Lake Timsah, whatever the religious requirements. I applied and was accepted.

The SSM was furious. I was his only touch typist, that's to say his fastest typist, and he did not want to lose me for a week. "You're a Scotsman; what do you want with the Church of England?" he said. His Sergeant nodded in agreement. My Pay Book gave my religion as Church of Scotland.

I took a chance that the two of them wouldn't know much about religion in Scotland. "Yes" I explained, "but I went to the Episcopal Church of Scotland (true, to play snooker on a Sunday) and it's in communion with the Church of England - and I've never been confirmed" (true, because confirmation doesn't exist in the Church of Scotland), so I didn't know what it was. But I was keen to find out, if it meant getting away to Lake Timsah for a while. A week later I set off, large pack on my back containing all I needed for a week's holiday, lots of Nivea cream, and some aspirins, plus I'd borrowed a bible from the Command Library, just in case.

On the first day at Lake Timsah I'd had a minor shock. Apparently it was necessary to be Baptised before one could be Confirmed. I had visions of being sent back in disgrace to 'G' Camp, of the SSM being triumphant. However, I was not the only one there in such an underprivileged condition. Five of us were marched down to the beach by the Padre; we were stood in the water, asked if we were prepared to accept the Christian religion, said 'Yes", had water poured over us, and were confirmed as ready for Confirmation later in the week.

Apart from the religion, the Lake Timsah course was all I'd hoped for. The would-be 'confirmists' were drawn from all camps and regiments in the Canal Zone. There were about 20 of us in all, some very keen on religion. I was the only one from our camp. We were in tented accommodation, 4 to a tent. Egyptian servants brought tea round in the mornings, HQ BTE it was not. The religion of the course took place in a small stone chapel, inland, a bit from the beach and behind our tents. Windows were small, high on walls painted a mat white. This provided a relatively cool space in contrast to the heat outside. In charge of the course was a very nice Major, a Padre from the Lancashire Fusiliers. Stockily built, he could have been a rugby fly-half, but he had a soft voice and an ingratiating manner. I felt he was a bit too nice for me ever to be at ease with him. He was very aware of his looks, and seemed to see himself as an Army poet and Padre. I'm not sure which of these was the more important to him.

After the morning's kneeling, praying, singing hymns, and a sermon in the Padre's mellifluous voice, we were all privileged with readings from some of his poems. We all listened attentively, some squirmed a bit, and I wasn't sure if some modest applause wasn't expected at the end. Selected paragraphs from Lady Chatterley were, of course, more to the taste of the average squaddie than selected poems, but here, apart from me, there was no average squaddies; most of the guys seemed genuinely religious. I found his poems rather strange; he seemed to be fascinated by conception, and the pregnancy cycle of women. A lot of his imagery had to do with the moment of birth, when the vagina burst open and the baby shot out, as he said "like a shell from a cannon". I didn't know much about childbirth, but I had a feeling it wasn't quite like that. I got the impression that some of the more religious guys were squirming a bit, embarrassed by it all.

Unlike the strict protocol of other officers, the Padre liked to join us at meal times and in the bar. At these times he reverted to officer type, in that he took it as his right to lead the conversation. As he led it into areas of religion, about which I knew nothing, I tried to keep myself in the background. Some of the others were very keen to discuss various concepts with him, and to me they seemed to be quite knowledgeable. Every afternoon we were on the beach, with football, cricket and beach tennis, or as much of these as the heat would allow. When we got too hot we went into the water, where at first, like one or two others on the course, I couldn't swim. Every afternoon the Padre appeared on the beach, tanned, muscular, hairy body in the slightest of slips. He was very keen to teach those of us who couldn't, to swim. On land he demonstrated the basic strokes, then in the shallows he held us up, rather too long for my liking, by chest and pelvis, supposedly until we got confidence in ourselves. I got confident quickly. I didn't like the touch of male hands on my body. I longed for the one piece woollen swimming costume that I loathed as a boy, when my granny knitted me it. I'm sure that it would have made me less attractive to hold. With the support of the heavily salted water of Lake Timsah I was soon swimming on my own, and floating. One could float on one's back for hours, and admire the giant cargo boats going through the adjacent Suez Canal. They towered above you, the height of a Glasgow tenement. A weird experience.

On return to 'G' Branch, I had to put up with a lot of ribaldry from my mates. Was I going to lead them in 'bedtime prayers'? Would I be wanting back my 'Lady Chatterley?' Could they swear in my presence? The SSM welcomed me back with a large pile of the Cornishman's work to be re-typed.

Round about the end of May we had to participate in our first proper Army Exercise. This was not of the order of the limited day and night exercises that we had done back in training at Aldershot, with the useless Lance Corporal Bastard Smith. Our SSM revelled in giving us all the details, trying to frighten us with stories of the use of live ammunition. "Not that you are going to be using it" he said, "but keep your heads down".

Apparently the camp was going to be attacked by the Welsh Guards, and defended by 16 Independent Parachute Brigade Group. For the exercise we were no longer going to be clerks and typists, but stand-in Infantrymen. We would be a second line of defence, grouped around the 'G' Branch complex of buildings. We would have to defend it against any Guardsmen who had managed to break through the Paras. As if. Anyway, we were all excited.

We were less excited when we discovered that the week before the exercise took place we had to sandbag all round our Branch enclosure. Not only that, we had to fill the bags ourselves with sand from the Sinai desert. All twelve of us, after breakfast, were loaded into a lorry and dumped with spades, bags, Sten guns and rifles in the desert. The sun was near it's zenith by this time, and here we were, stripped to the waist, no longer 'pinkos', shovelling up sand and sweating profusely, with a pail of hot tea to slake our thirsts. It did occur to me again, that in building Moascar the Army had pushed the desert back, and here we were now bringing it back into Moascar in bags. We felt very exposed in this situation; the lorry had departed back to camp, and we were alone, surrounded by sand dunes for as far as the eye could see.

Our Corporal in charge avoided any of the hard work by patrolling around us with his Sten gun. "My duty is to get you all back in one piece" he said, pretentiously. He managed this in time for lunch, then he oversaw us sandbagging around the Branch. Relieved of his sentry duties, he was still un-inclined towards manual labour.

On the morning of the exercise, Ron, Ray and I were ensconced behind the sandbagged entry to the Branch. We were there to defend it with Bren, Sten and several rounds of blank ammunition against the Welsh Guards, should they break through the Paras' line, which was unlikely. We had a spirit stove with which we kept ourselves going with hot tea, played cards, and watched what we could see of the action through our binoculars. It wasn't a lot. We could hear lots of gunfire, see flares going off, smell cordite and had our eyes nipped by the fumes blowing our way from smoke bombs. Lots of marshals with their referees' yellow arm bands passed in Land Rovers. A visiting General arrived in a Staff car to liaise with our Colonel. We took great delight in stopping his car and demanding his papers. Lounging in the back of his Super Snipe it was difficult to see if he was impressed or annoyed by our action.

Late in the afternoon a siren went off to mark the end of the exercise. The Paras had held their line, we were told by a passing marshal, so we could all relax. We dismounted the Bren and laid aside the Stens and ammunition. The cook house had sent across some sandwiches and a pail of tea, as there would be no dinner that night. We were eating, laughing and drinking, totally relaxed, when a group of disgruntled Welsh Guards appeared on the road passing the Branch. We gave them a friendly wave and in return they threw us a lit thunder-flash, which landed on top of the sandbags spluttering and sparking. They laughed. Briefed by Biggles and the Boys Own stories, I knew what to do. I leant forward to pick it up and throw it back before it exploded. It exploded. I was blind and deaf, but most of all worried about what my granny was going to say when she got me back as a total liability for the rest of her life. She'd known the Army was wrong for me. She was right. My mates caught me before I fell, dragged me into the Branch and sat me on a chair. They bathed my eyes with warm water, and the SSM dug into his safe and produced a bottle of brandy. He reluctantly forced several tea-spoons of it into my mouth. I recovered sight, sound and speech in a few minutes, but eyebrows, eyelashes and frontal hair took several weeks to reappear.

Even as clerks we were expected to keep up our rifle practice. Once a month we were timetabled, with the out-postings from the infantry and paras that shared our barracks, to be on the rifle range. But in our 19 months in Egypt, we only had one visit to the rifle range. I think that our SSM and Colonel had made a case with the Camp Commandant to have us relieved of this duty, on the grounds of necessity to have the General's Branch fully staffed with the rising terrorist action. The month after the exercise in which the Welsh Guards had blown off my eyebrows and eyelashes, we had an early breakfast and were bussed in the relative cool of the morning, with assorted infantrymen, mechanics, engineers and paras, to the rifle range in the desert to the west of Moascar. This range was something that the Army had constructed in the middle of the dessert. It consisted of the usual line or firing positions 200, 400 and 600 yards away, the three distances being stepped above each other, as at Aldershot. But here in the Egyptian sun, it was necessary to have a roof of bamboo extending above the firing positions to give shade, and level with the ground another such roof the length of the markers' trench. The baffle wall behind the targets was covered in sand bags, themselves covered by the ever-shifting sands of the desert The range of the Lee-Enfield .303 bullet was over a mile, so this wall was designed to stop the bullets travelling that far and hitting any stray Arabs and camels wandering amongst the sand dunes. It also had a use for the local community that we were to find out about later.

We were split into four groups of 12, 2 groups went off to man the butts, the targets, and the rest stayed at the firing positions. Once the targets were raised, and the Sergeant in charge of the butts team had indicated his team were ready, the red flag would be raised as a warning to all that firing was about to commence. The first 12 then lay down and commenced firing. Unlike at Aldershot we were not beginners, and we were not all in the same platoon. There was not the same comradeship between the shooters, and not the same average ability. The infantrymen and paras went professionally about their business of hitting bulls and inners, so were left to their own devices by the gunnery Sergeants. The mechanics, engineers and us clerks were given advice on our lying positions, our sight adjustment, and reminded to "hold your breath and squeeze, not pull the trigger". This was not said without the odd swear word, but was much more sympathetic than the gunnery Sergeants at Aldershot, and I'm sure the marksmanship improved as a result. Still, not much was expected of us as marksmen, but when one of my mates nicked a bull, the watching Sergeant shouted to all in the line admiringly, "fuck me we're going to have to transfer this guy to the infantry!" Ray missed the target with his next shot; there was no way he wanted to swap his cosy office number to spend the rest of his service in infantry training, marching, arms-drill, assault courses and rifle range.

Once we'd fired off our 6 rounds 'in our own time', then the six rounds rapid fire, the green flag was raised at the butts. There was a period of half an hour's peace as targets were repaired and we changed our positions from firing to marking. On our way to the butts, we all noticed half a dozen Arabs, flitting like white moths in their djeballas behind the targets, in front of the barrier wall behind. They were searching feverishly, sifting through the sand, for our spent bullets. These little bits of metal could be exchanged by them for money in the Ismailiya souk or bazaar. Our Sergeant said that this was a regular occurrence; these poor Arabs appeared whenever the rifle range was in use. Most of us were appalled that poverty could reduce humans to take such risks for so little, but some sniggered "why don't we use them for target practice?" then added "just a joke", on seeing the abhorrence on our faces. At noon the lorries arrived to take us back to camp and lunch. We had sore shoulders; the Lee-Enfield still had a kick like a horse, but it had been a good morning's break from office work. Good practice too, lots of inners from the non-infantry men, and Ray's bull. Officers and NCOs were reasonably happy on the way back. But I couldn't forget these white moths of Arabs, hunting for their wee bits of metal. That anyone should be that poor and desperate depressed me.

A week after the shoot the new bike was delivered. It had bright red paint, a lovely soft comfortable saddle, and shiny chrome upright handlebars with good brakes. We were all delighted with it. It was so un-army looking, and unlike the old one it ran quietly and smoothly, as we found out riding it round the Branch. Even the Cornishman could ride it. For some reason the SSM was not pleased. He made a phone call. The next morning a Quartermaster Corporal arrived, and took the new bike away. We were all furious, and asked the SSM "Why?" He smiled, inclined his head in the annoying way he had, and said nothing; he was good at that type of thing. A week later the bike was back, all covered in matt sand coloured paint. It was now an Army bike. It still ran smoothly and quietly though. The SSM gave the old one to his house-boy.

One morning I came into the Branch and had difficulty in understanding what the SSM was saying to me.

It wasn't his Brummie accent, I'd deciphered that the first week I was there. I definitely wasn't hearing him very well. I turned my attention to the Cornishman. He might have been slow, but he spoke with a cut glass accent. He was the only farmer's son that I knew (I knew a few of them, from being evacuated during the second world war, to the farming village of Balfron) who'd gone to a private (or as he called it, public) school. I'd gone to one of these public schools myself, but it hadn't taught me received pronunciation. Anyway, I couldn't hear the Cornishman either. I barely made out a loud bark from the SSM.

"Private Nelson, are you going deaf?"

"I think I am, sir".

"Go right now to the MO (Medical Officer) and get your ears syringed out, that's an order".

"Right away, sir". Any excuse to get away from the Branch for an hour or so. I remembered that my grand-dad had his ears syringed out twice a year. So the wax build-up in my ears was genetic.

The MO turned out to be a Lieutenant from the Parachute Regiment. He was from Glasgow and we liked each other. There was no 'officer other rank' Queen's Regulations, distance between us. He told me he was being demobbed from this "fucking Army" in a few months. He hated the Parachute Regiment, wished he'd never volunteered for it.

"Why did you?" I asked.

"Always fancied parachuting" he said. "Liked the idea of viewing a panorama of the countryside while floating gently down to earth. Didn't realise I'd have to take all that shit at Officer Training from these thick Sergeants. The square bashing, the arms drill, the bloody officers' mess, I hate it all...well no, I liked the parachuting. I'll join a club when I get home." He inspected my ears, confirmed I needed them syringed out and handed me over to an orderly.

My ears syringed out I thanked the orderly, didn't hear what he said in reply, and left the MO's quarters into the 90 odd degree sun to make my way back to 'G' Branch. I noticed that none of the birds were singing or the crickets chirping. Back at my desk the SSM silently threw down a pile of typing and I saw his lips moving. I heard nothing, nobody; I was now totally deaf.

"I've got to go back to the MO's" I'd apparently shouted as, clamping beret on head I rushed out.

"You're ears are really blocked now" said the MO. Taking me through to the orderly's room, he demanded of him, "What did you use to syringe this man's ears out with?"

"Water, sir" was the answer.

"Hot or cold?"

"Err..cold sir".

"Idiot. Do it again with hot water".

I walked back to the Branch, whistling in tune with the birds. In the Branch I could hear a pin drop but unfortunately the SSM's remarks, orders and asides were several octaves higher than normal.

Around this time some of the lads decided to be real soldiers and get tattooed. Tattooing was popular in Egypt for religious, weddings and other purposes. Usually, however, it was done with henna dyes, no skin pricking, and therefore not permanent. But a permanent option was possible, and this was what some of the lads wanted. I wanted none of it however. My grandparents were of the opinion that a tattoo marked one out as a rather 'common' person, and it was only, but barely, acceptable in sailors and old soldiers. Certainly my grand-uncle RSM Jock Buchanan didn't have one, and it was unknown among any of their other friends or acquaintances. Anyway, I didn't fancy having my skin permanently marked by some image I knew that I would grow tired of in time. Some of the guys went ahead and had them, usually nostalgic images of mums, girlfriends, football teams, or their town or country of origin. My friend George's was an anthem to Newcastle United. I didn't like the results. The colours seemed to be mostly indigo, and the drawings I thought were poor. Some guys had the name of their fiancé tattooed on their arm, only to receive later a 'dear John' letter, telling them that the engagement was off. They were very upset, but on getting over it, they pinned such letters on the NAAFI notice board for all to see. Publicising their loss seemed to have a cathartic effect on their grief, but it didn't remove the evidence of a lost love from their arms.

We were moving towards the end of the year. A football match was arranged between the Scots and the English. My fellow countrymen seemed to have overlooked my last sad performance as a goalkeeper. They asked me to play in goal again — for the English.

The sky was overcast, warm and no rain. There was no need here in Egypt, for the Christmas and New Year swapping of duties between Scots and Anglos, as there had been in training at Aldershot. No-one was going home from HQ BTE. We were all looking forward to the Christmas dinner, which traditionally would be served to us by officers and senior NCOs. Christmas day came, and we were all sat down in the command dining hall at long trestle tables. There were fancy hats, crackers and free bottles of beer. The Catering Corps cooks had done a good job. Turtle soup, turkey, Brussel sprouts and bread sauce. Apart from eating off a worn pine table, and sitting on a bench, it was just like home, except I couldn't eat the Christmas pudding. Unlike my granny, the Army cooks didn't do puddings without eggs. There were no alternatives so I just did without as allergies were not in the remit of the Catering Corps. I wondered at the time who was going to cook the cooks' Christmas dinner? We were waited on by senior NCOs and Second Lieutenants; senior officers wandered around in the background, talking to each other, drinking whisky to our beer, and occasionally giving an order to the waiters. The head of the 'G' Staff, our acting Colonel Stevens, gave a motivational speech.

Apparently we'd all done well this year, and he expected us to do as much again next year. Then he offered a toast to the Queen, at which we all stood to attention, some reluctantly, glass in hand. After the toast Turkish coffee was served, and conversations became animated. Free beer continued to flow, and it was obvious that some spirits had been smuggled in. Noise increased, the festive spirit was now being fuelled by whisky. Things were getting rowdy. Having no doubt seen it all before, the Colonel, officers and Warrant officers now moved off to the safety of their respective messes. My pals and I left before the Guard was turned out to quell the punch-ups. The Colour Sergeant had the remains of a plate of turtle soup emptied over his head, and down his red sash. Several well-known faces were, from then on, seen only on the tea run until the middle of January.

It was now the New Year. The Cornishman and I were on Branch duty on Hogmanay till New Year's day. That the SSM chose to pair me, the only Scotsman in the Branch, with his least useful Private, on the main night on the Scottish calendar, did not endear him to me. Around midnight there was a series of bangs. I took them to be the off-duty guys letting off fireworks to cel-ebrate the New Year. Then I remembered I was not in Glasgow, and fireworks were banned in Army Egypt so as not to be confused with terrorist fire into the camp. It was terrorist fire into the camp. It seemed to be very close to our roof. We lay down on the floor. I started to crawl towards the safe that held our weapons, but then the thought of putting a loaded gun in the hands of the Cornishman, with me close beside him, changed my mind. I'd probably be in more danger from him armed, than from a terrorist. I reminded him that it was his turn, if any messages came through, of cut oil pipe lines or whatever, to take them to the General's house; before the firing I'd done several visits while he'd been asleep. He said he couldn't, that while he'd learnt to ride the Branch bike in day time, he couldn't do it in the dark. If only the Branch had had a tractor instead of a bicycle.

Chapter 3

HAGGIS IN THE SOUP

In our barrack room only Ron, Ray, Sandy the Cornishman and myself were from the Service Corps. The rest were from many sources, Pay Corps, cooks and some infantrymen, outsourced to us from their regiments, for some reason or another. They were employed in our camp as firemen, camp orderlies, regimental policemen, bin-men and general handymen.

One Northern Irishman took great delight in telling us that he was a Republican supporter of the IRA. On being asked why he was in the British Army and had taken an oath to serve the Queen, he replied:

"Well, there is no work in Northern Ireland, and here I have free board and lodgings for the next two years, and I'm paid into the bargain". Then he grinned sardonically, "and the arms training will be useful when the revolution comes".

"You'll be dead by then", he was told, "or you'll be in the Glass House".

A Pay Corps Corporal spent much of his time off duty lounging on his bed, reading and laughing. This wasn't usual among the squaddies, so intrigued, I asked him the cause of his merriment.

"P.G. Woodhouse" he replied, showing me his book. I read a few paragraphs and was immediately enthralled by the world of Jeeves and Wooster. He lent me some of their books, I read them, returned them for him to the Command Library, and borrowed a few of their extensive stock for myself. Wooster and Jeeves gave me much laughter over the years, well beyond the period of my National Service.

My pal in the Pay Corps was made up to a Sergeant mid-October, and had left our billet for the adjoining room. He was demobbed at the end of January. Two days later a new Sergeant appeared in our billet. He was small, tanned, wiry, and on the sleeve of his jacket wore the badge of 16 Independent Parachute Brigade Group.

"Silence, you men" he bellowed, getting our reluctant attention. "I'm Sergeant Wein, your Sergeant in charge, next door". He nodded to his room, then added with a scowl, "I'm a bastard, a hard bastard, so don't push your luck".

He looked a bastard, so we wouldn't push our luck. Wein was not a bastard like Substantive Private Bastard Corporal Smith back in Aldershot. He only swore at us with reasonable reason now and again. Why he'd been out-posted from the Paras we'd never know. He claimed he'd coached the Paras' boxing team and we believed him. Now he was starting up a boxing team in our camp, at all weights. He was enthusiastic, we weren't, but he was a determined wee man. His method of recruitment was to come into our billet of an afternoon, when we were all relaxing after work and lunch, lying on our beds, reading, writing, polishing boots, sleeping or contemplating life after National Service. He would start open-handed sparring with one of us. Open-handed was very sore, when you were poked in the face or ribs with his iron finger tips. Very few of us liked it; if you fought back with any skill, you were in his boxing team. If you didn't, you were treated to one of his rare swears, "you're a fucking pussy; you should be in the WRACS". I'd seen a few women in the Women's Royal Army Corps who should have been in the Paras.

When he started on me I gave as good as I got. When I'd entered Secondary School, I was off a lot with my asthma. My uncle Peter, an amateur boxer with the Boys Brigade, decided that I needed to learn his sport to fend off school bullies who imagined that a child with health problems would be an easy target. From then on I wasn't. Also in Secondary School, I had a classmate, one Dick Currie, who was later to win the Golden Gloves at fly-weight in the USA, before turning professional, with rather less success. At school he and I sparred open-handed regularly.

Sergeant Wein was delighted by my speed and accuracy in attack and counter-punching. "Get you fighting fit (different from Army fit) and you'll make an excellent featherweight" he said.

I had no intention of going into his boxing team; I didn't fancy trying to dodge for 3 rounds the punches of some elite Army boxer. A wee guy from Paisley, also outsourced from the Paras, had flattened me a few times in our friendly sparring. He was to go on to be a key member of Wein's team.

Within a month the boxing team of Moascar Garrison was up and running. We were awakened in the morning by their training runs. Led by Sergeant Wein, with noisy encouragement from his heavyweight, one of our Regimental Policemen, they were out on the road at 6 a.m., passing below our windows running and grunting, while we moaned to each other at being awakened. Another month and a ring was erected in the middle of the football pitch. Chairs and benches were placed around it for spectators. We all sat there one hot night in February, to support our boys in their first fight. They did well against the Lancashire Fusiliers. My Paisley buddy was a star, knocking his man out in the first round. Our Heavyweight RP did the same. Wein had actually managed to recruit a National Service Second Lieutenant, who'd learnt the noble art at Eton, or some such English private school. We all liked him. He was tall, good looking, and had a good attitude to Other Ranks; that was us. His dark thick hair was worn, non-regulation, down to his collar, so he was a bit of a rebel. All that went down well with the 'hoi polloi'. Unfortunately Army boxing was not Eton boxing. His opponent had never heard of the Marquis of Queensbury, or his rules. He didn't last out the 3 rounds, and that was his last fight for Wein. Our team did well in later fights, against the HLI, the Engineers and the Pioneers. I was Branch Duty Clerk the night when they met

Wein's old team, the Paras. The next day I learned that there had been a massacre; they were all beaten except for the wee hard man from Paisley, himself a para.

Personnel in the barrack room changed from time to time. Some were demobbed, some were transferred to other units, and some, usually regular soldiers, were promoted to Sergeant. Sergeants were roomed in twos, next to the billets. Somebody went, and a new Corporal appeared in our room. He was a small smarmy type, who spent most of his time writing letters to his mother, washing his socks and blancoing his stripes. Unfortunately he inherited the empty bed next to mine. One Sunday pm when we were all relaxing, reading, lying about on beds, playing cards, polishing bits of equipment or sleeping, he began setting up an ironing board between our beds. I was happily reading Wooster's problem with his love for the lady captain of his golf club, when the ironer, spreading a shirt on his board, and grinning all over his face, said 'Wot you readin' 'Aggis?' My mates called me 'Lindlay', and some Englishmen followed their nation's Imperial laziness in calling me 'Jock'. I didn't mind the 'Jock', though I couldn't fathom what it was with the English, with their desire to call all other nationals by names such as 'Jock', 'Taffy' and 'Paddy'; not much of a stretch from calling all Arabs 'Wogs'. It wasn't only the intellectually challenged that reverted to the generic 'Jock'. One of our Majors in 'G Operations' was an Englishman co-opted from the Highland Light Infantry (City of Glasgow Regiment, hardly Highland), perhaps because he was intelligent enough to be a General's Staff major, or because he was too fat to be of any use to the HLI. He made a habit of referring to me as

'Jock', rather than the regulation Private Nelson. Mindful of his regiment's and my Glasgow origins, when there was any straffing of the camp by Egyptian terrorists, he'd advise me to go and get my 'razor'. I'd smile wanly and go off and get my Sten gun.

I was brought out of this reverie by a loud 'Do you 'Aggises' ave any books up there in 'Aggisland?' I was aware that this 'Haggis' caller, being a Corporal, had to be dealt with differently from my first such problem back in training camp. It was a two-way thing of course; being a Corporal he, according to Queen's Regulations, should have been showing respect to an 'other rank' under his command, and calling me 'Private Nelson'. He was a dim little bugger though, having signed on for 3 years instead of 2, and already regretting it. That was probably the reason he was made up to Corporal; we certainly couldn't discern any other reasons for his rank. So I decided that I'd better play this carefully and diplomatically. I explained to him that I didn't like to be called 'Haggis'. He could call me 'Private Nelson', as regulations required or, as we were all in the same barrack room, he could be less official and call me 'Lindlay', as the Pay Corps Corporal did. Neither did I mind too much being called 'Jock'.

He listened with a supercilious smile, and said "Is that right, Haggis?"

I grabbed him by the throat and said "I'll do you in, you little bastard, if you call me that again".

Wriggling to get out of my grasp, red faced and choking, he lisped out "Yyyyou're on a charge...attacking a

Corporal, you you're... on a charge, Nelson". Aghast at my temper and stupidity, I let him go. Turning to the other grinning occupants of the room, he choked 'You're all witnesses, you saw Nelson attack me".

"No we didn't" they all said, well, except for one little shit of a friend of his. God I thought, I'm going to be on a charge, on Company Orders, in front of the Camp Commander and the RSM, on a charge of attacking an NCO. I'm going to be in the Guard House for weeks, on the tea run, sandwiched between two regimental police-men, trying to keep in step with their Light Infantry march. 'I'll be having my heels kicked, my toes stubbed, slops from the two heavy pails of tea will be burning my legs. Off the tea run I'll be at the mercy of the sadistic tendencies of the RP's for every menial job in the guard house, latrine cleaning, taking out the bins etc. All because I can't keep my temper in the face of some dim wit's imagined demeaning of me. All I could see was a dark tunnel leading me to the Guard House for several weeks. There was no light at the end of that tunnel. No hope for me at all. No light at all, oh wait a minute, was that a glow? Yes it was, and I began to smile. My smile grew.

The more my smile grew, the more annoyed the half throttled one became. Turning over his shirt he spat out at me, 'You won't be fucking smiling Private Nelson (Private Nelson? He didn't want throttled again) when I have you up in front of the Commanding Officer and RSM on a charge of attacking an NCO. 'Oh I don't know', I said I might be smiling when you charge me in front of kilt wearing Commanding Officer Lachlan

MacDonald of the Argyll and Sutherland Highlanders, and tartan trew wearing RSM Alastair Fairlie of the Royal Scots.

Our fracas had broken the boredom of a Sunday afternoon for the other residents of the billet, who in the main were not friendly to our new corporal. There was great glee at his discomfort, shouts for me to finish him off, and one delighted shout of 'fuck me the stupid little bastard's going to charge the Haggis in front of the Haggises! The stupid little bastard's face began to pucker, I thought he was going to cry, laying down his iron, he quickly left the room, hastily followed by his weasel witness.

A great feeling of relief swept through me, mates in the room hailed my triumph. An acrid smell entered my nostrils. I lent forward and lifted the iron from the corporal's shirt, where it had left across the pay book pocket, a silhouette in burnt umber of a tiny rowing boat.

My birthday was at the beginning of April, but it was much later that my cards and presents arrived from home. I was somewhat dismayed to find an 'Episcopalian Church of Scotland' Hymn Book as my present from Ina, my fiancé. What the hell was I going to do with that? I wasn't religious. I didn't go to church, except when I got a chance of a holiday at Lake Timsah out of it, or a game of snooker back at Ina's church in Glasgow. A hymn book to me didn't make for good bed time reading either, being neither exciting or amusing. D.H. Lawrence and P.G. Wodehouse were very much preferable. I didn't think of myself as an atheist, as my father had been, but church was boring, and I didn't believe in prayer.

During World War II I'd prayed constantly to God to let Scotland beat England at football. He hadn't listened to me. Either he was English or, as my grandfather said, the War Office had kept the best English footballers at home, and sent the best Scots abroad. Whatever, a hymn book was not a present I wanted, and it made me wonder if I was right to consider marrying someone who'd think I'd want such a present.

By May the Egyptian summer was well on its way. Temperatures were nicely into the nineties. It was hot, dry, and the winds which blew in from the desert were like the opening of a hot oven door. 15 months here and not a drop of rain. Then one day on our way back from the dining hall at lunch time, it suddenly got very dark. Before we could reach the shelter of our building, water fell on us from above. Rain. Rain, heavy, straight down in rods, such as I had never ever experienced in Glasgow. Unlike Glasgow, there were no gutters or road drains to cope with this phenomena. The road was flooded, and by the time we reached our room, our shirts, shorts and socks were soaked through. After all the unbearable heat, this dampness was fresh and cooling. We stood around the room, shaking off the wet and laughing, drying ourselves, and looking from our balcony at the unbelievable torrent of rain from the heavens.

There was an almighty bang, and the door to our billet flew open and hit the wall. Standing there was Sergeant

Wein, puce of face, and wet from head to foot. Some of the water was being absorbed by his hastily pulled on shorts. Water dripping from his sturdy hairy legs, was pooling on the floor at his feet. We all stood looking, paralysed, like rabbits in the headlights of an oncoming car.

"Which of you fucking bastards cut the lead off my roof?" A giggle was hastily stifled. "Fucking trouser weights; I'll give you buggers trouser weights. I want all your bloody weights out on your beds NOW".

Ronnie and me exchanged fearful looks. This was it, our number was up. Guard House for a fortnight, delivering tea, having our ankles kicked by Regimental Policemen making us march faster than was our norm. All weights were dug out of our bedside wardrobes, and laid out on our beds, except for the Cornishman, whose creased trousers bore witness both to his uselessness with an iron, and to his lack of weights. Wein, barefoot and dripping water over the floor, started at the bed on the right hand side of the door. We were on the left hand side, and would be last to be inspected. The wait to learn our fate was horrible. The first weights to be looked at were those of a dour Welshman, who normally only conversed after his third pint. His weights were lead wrapped around a bit of rope.

"Where did you get this fucking lead, Private Jones?" We couldn't believe that Jones, the Jonah of the room, was getting all of us off the hook.

"Handed to me by a soldier mate, going home on demob, Sergeant" Jones replied.

As Wein moved round the room it became apparent that all of us had been the beneficiaries of demob-happy men. Before he got to Ron and me, he gave up, but not without dire threats. "Right, you bastards, I'll be watching you all from now on. Break one fucking regulation, and I'll have you running with my boxing team at 6 a.m. every morning until your demob. Don't fucking think I'm kidding."

We didn't. We later learnt that he'd been sleeping off his night duty as Sergeant of the Guard, when the only rain in the Canal Zone in our time, was to come through his roof and soak him as he lay asleep in his bed.

Despite my discontent with Ina's birthday present to me, I kept her framed photo on my bedside table. At the beginning of our service most of the bedside tables were similarly decorated with photos of loved ones back home. Now, due to 'Dear John' letters there were fewer. One day, coming back from lunch, I discovered a six foot tall, long, skinny, loose limbed, loose mouthed guy, by the name of Forrest sitting on my bed. He was writing a letter on my bedside table, with Ina's photo face down. He was an infantryman out-posted with a pal from the HLI at Tel el Kebir. He was a strange guy who would parade around the barrack room in the nude on occasion. This was to best display his penis, the longest that anyone of us had ever seen. He was obviously very proud of it.

I was reminded of the Glasgow playground jingle, 'long and thin goes too far in, and doesn't please the ladies, Short and thick, it does the trick, and manufactures babies'. Those of us of lesser endowment (all) consoled ourselves that he never had, or would, get it up; it was slack like the rest of him. His pal was the opposite size and shape from him, being short and fat. They were both buddies from Paisley and were employed permanently on sanitary duties around our camp. They spent most of their time in denim fatigues, which he was wearing as he sat on my bed. Both these guys didn't mix well with the rest of the billet, kept to themselves, and on their days off dressed up in their kilts, and went off by Army bus into Fayed. Why Fayed? No one knew. What was there in Fayed to attract them? It was an RAF town, and two soldiers in kilts would be the butt of Air Force humour. These two were not the types to handle this too well. So why go there? We were to find out later.

Meanwhile I was just annoyed to see latrine fatigues mucking up my bed, then I noticed that his own bed was covered by his kilt, sporran and all the rest of the HLI dress uniform, so I guessed that this was their afternoon for a visit to Fayed. Putting on my best Glasgow hard man accent I said, "Gonna get aff ma bed!"

His long pasty face looked up at me and he said "When ah hiv finished ma letter!"

"Naw" I said. "Now!" I grabbed him by his dirty shirt and yanked him up with difficulty. He threw a punch at me which I parried easily, and punched him twice in the stomach. My uncle Peter had always recommended this as the best attack to end a fight quickly. He fell forward, and I tried to get out of his way. I didn't, and as he fell he grabbed me round the legs, and we fell to the floor. This was not the type of fight that I wanted. I didn't want a wrestling match. With my feet off the ground

I couldn't get any weight behind my punches, which were now landing ineffectually on his side and back ribs, and I began to realise that he was stronger than I thought he was.

Most of the guys in the room were now yelling me on to finish him off. He wasn't popular, but their support was of no avail to me as we rolled around the floor; it was like wrestling an octopus. I could feel my punches getting weaker, and his crushing arms getting stronger, and I feared another humiliation coming my way. I tried a Glasgow kiss, but only hit his chin and hurt my forehead. Saved by the bell. My supporters suddenly went silent.

"Get up off the bloody floor, you two!" Sergeant Wein had entered the room and was standing over us. "Get up, Private Forrest, Private Nelson, or you're on a charge!" Arms were disentangled and the better relieved of the two of us, I dusted myself down. "If you want to fight I'll take you down to the gym; you'll put on the gloves and I'll referee". Wein turned to the skinny one "Want to do that now?"

Big as he was, there was no way he was going to win a boxing match, so he said "Naw!"

Wein looked at me and said "Nelson (lack of the 'Private' marked a thaw in his attitude to me), you could do with some toughening up. Come down to the gym and join the boxing team?"

I felt grateful to him for saving me, so l said "I'll think about it". It didn't take much thought; boxing Forrest was one thing, getting into the ring with a sadistic Army bruiser was something else entirely. Wein forced us to shake hands, which we did glumly. Forrest returned to his own bed, I retrieved Ina's photo and replaced it in its place of honour. As I took off my top bedsheet for dhobbying, I was offered helpful advice as to how I could have won the day. "Kick him in the balls!" was the favourite. Forrest and his mate put on their kilts and disappeared in the direction of Fayed, for whatever purpose only they, at that moment knew.

At the end of May, with the sun high in the sky but not yet too hot, the Army Egypt Rifle Shoot competition was to take place. The organisation of this was the responsibility of 'G' Training. That is to say, Major Malcolm, the Colonel, and with Private Nelson to do all the drudgery of typing, posting and answering the phone. The Colonel kept the Major straight on all executive matters, and I made sure that he remembered appointments and so forth. This was second nature to me. The Major had a lot in common with my errant father, who also forgot appointments and obligations. Given a letter to post by my granny, my father would put it in his jacket pocket. It would stay there for a month, and then be sent to the cleaners with the jacket. The Major was of that ilk.

The Rifle Competition was to be held at the rifle butts in Fayed. The Royal Engineers had prepared a large stretch of the desert looking towards the butts, for spectators. The Major had to make a trip through there to inspect the work in progress. A bank of scaffolding was being erected to provide seating for the Colonels, officers, senior NCO's and wives. There was also a special podium on which Lieutenant General Festing would present the medals to the winners. To the left of the bank of seats and rifle range, there was a long strip of ground which was being levelled by bulldozers. This was to be the airstrip on which the General would land, shortly before the presentation of the medals. There were also arrayed around the seating area various stalls, where one could buy sandwiches, hot dogs and sweets. For the officers, warrant officers and wives, there was a restaurant tent, with a menu of 3 course meals and wine. For us, all ranks below Sergeant, there was a large tent inside which there were tables, seats, a coffee counter and bar. The Army Egypt Rifle Shoot was to be a carnival occasion enjoyed by all.

The great day arrived, not yet too hot. There was great excitement in the Branch; we were all going to the Rifle Shoot, except for one disgruntled Major, a Corporal and my mate Ronnie Ross. They were being left in charge of the Branch for the day. From our camp RSM Fairlie, our boxing Second lieutenant, and a Regimental Policeman had all qualified for the Shoot. Early in the morning, while the Major was at 'Colonel's prayers', a heavy pine box was delivered to me by dispatch rider, all the way from a silversmith in Cairo. Inside the box were the medals, resting on purple silk. Ribbons were in a separate package, red for first, blue second and white third. I threaded all the ribbons through the medals, so they were ready for immediate presentation. It would be the Major's job to hand them to the General in the right order. I replaced everything carefully in the box, and placed it on the centre of the Major's desk, with a large notice saying 'Medals'.

Around noon, with packed lunches, we were all ready to leave. The Branch NCOs and privates were going in a bus, and the Colonel, Major and other officers with their wives in the luxury fleet of Humber Super Snipe Staff cars, pennants flying from their front wings. I was required to be with the Major, as his secretary, but not too close to him. No luxury ride in a Staff car for me. I was sat between two Sten gun carrying MPs in the back of one of the angle iron escorting Land Rovers. It wasn't comfortable. On arrival at the Shoot site, the Major and officers had their lunch ready for them in their restaurant. We ate our sandwiches and had cups of tea in the café tent. As shooting commenced, the Major, fellow officers and wives or girlfriends, took their places on the bank of seats. I was required to make myself permanently available nearby. I got a chair from the café and sat myself down in the shade of the scaffolding, to read my latest Jeeves and Wooster, in the clear site of Major Malcom. The afternoon wore on very pleasantly in the sun and heat, to the sound of gunfire, the smell of cordite and the shouts of the organising Sergeants and officers.

As the shoot was nearing its end, the Major indicated to me to come forward. I did. "I need the medals now, Nelson" he whispered.

"You've got them, sir" I said. "I left them on your table, for you to pick up before we left".

His normally tanned face went white. He'd forgotten them. He muttered to me, so the others couldn't hear, "Christ Nelson, we've forgotten the bloody things".

No, I thought. *Not we; you've forgotten them.*

Taking me by the arm he moved me to where the other officers couldn't see or hear him. He whispered, "the General's due in an hour, and no bloody medals." Face getting paler and paler, he could see his career ending in ignominy. General, no medals. Sent back to New Zealand, marked by the British Army as a failure. Brain dead from worrying about the looming disaster, all he could mutter was, "What can we do?".

Indeed, what could we do? It seemed pretty obvious to me. "I'll go back to Moascar and collect them. If the General arrives early, keep him talking till I get back".

A little colour returned to his face. "You think you can make it in time, Nelson?"

"Give me a Staff car and a fast driver and I will".

Relief flooded into his face, and with it, a return to officer status. "You can't have a Staff car, Private Nelson. I'll give you a chitty for a Land Rover, and a direction to the driver to drive fast".

So I found myself in the front seat of a Land Rover, the driver's Sten gun across my knees. As we drove I began to think, *was it my fault that the medals were forgotten?*

Should I have taken them? No. The place for the medals was on the leather seat of a Staff car, between the Major and the Colonel. We made fast time along the tree-lined Sweet Water Canal road. Myth had it, that if you fell into the ill-named Sweet Water, you'd need 12 inoculations when you came out, if you wanted to survive.

The disgruntled Corporal left behind at the Branch, cheered up a bit when I told him the story of the forgotten medals. He opened Major Malcolm's room. There they were, the medals, in the middle of his desk, with my note on top. I grabbed them and rushed back to the Land Rover. As we entered the car park at the Fayed butts, the General's Lysander was coming in to land. The anxious Major was in a group of officers waiting to greet him.

I marched up, saluted and said "the medals, sir."

"Put them on the Podium, Private Nelson" he said, haughtily dismissing me, for the benefit of his fellow officers.

The Shoot ended well for HQ BTE. RSM Fairlie won a gold and the Second Lieutenant won silver. Obviously there was far less difference between firing for the Rifle Club at Eton and firing for the Army than there was between Boxing for Eton and boxing for the Army. The Regimental Policeman won a Bronze. Not bad for a Headquarters Company. 42 Royal Marine Commando took the team prize, with 16 Independent Parachute Brigade Group second. The Durham Light Infantry edged out the Cameronians by a point for third. This did not go down well with the Cameronians; they were a rifle regiment after all. However, after the event they all retired to the Fayed NAAFI where they all, for a time, enjoyed an amicable pint together. The HLI had put on their kilts for the presentation and entered the NAAFI with them on. There was drinking of toasts between fighting men, all very friendly. As time wore on there were further regimental contests, for the quick downing of pints, arm wrestling etc.

Then an English voice loudly enquired of a mate, "Have you ever seen such a fucking ugly crowd of WRACS?" He wasn't looking at the few WRACS who were there; they were all quite pretty, made up nicely for the occasion. He was looking at the HLI. The HLI had been here before. The offending male was downed, mates went to his aid. It was DLI versus HLI. But fighting men, as we'd all been told we were on being enlisted, weren't going to miss the chance of a punch-up, certainly not after a few drinks. When the Lancashire Fusiliers joined the DLI, the HLI was outnumbered. The Cameronians, despite having a large proportion of Anglos, went to the aid of the HLI. The Paras, overwhelmingly English, joined their neighbours at Tel el Kabir garrison, the HLI. Seeing the choice of the Paras, the Commandos evened things up by joining the DLI. Late at night the MPs arrived, waited until everyone was exhausted, then arrested as many as they could get into their Land Rovers. We, the HQ BTE group, had had the foresight to leave before things got nasty, that is except for our out-sourced paras. They arrived back in camp the next afternoon with black eyes, cut lips and swollen fists, but all present and correct, ready for duty, as though nothing untoward had happened. For them, it probably hadn't.

I'd had very little problem in the Army with my egg allergy, until one morning on entering the cook house late with Sandy, after our night duty in G Branch. The cooks clearing up after breakfast, were never particularly pleased to see us late-comers off night duty. We were told that there was only scrambled eggs left for breakfast. This was okay for Sandy, and he went off to a table to eat his. Reminded of my egg allergy the cook grumbled away about it having nothing to do with him. He disappeared into the kitchen, and reappeared a few minutes later with a steaming plate of white and green stuff that even a rabid Celtic supporter would have baulked at. It didn't look nice, it didn't smell nice, and I was sure that it wouldn't taste nice.

"What is it?" I asked.

"Mashed potatoes and cabbage" the cook replied.

"For breakfast?" I asked.

"It's all that's left" he said.

"I'm not eating that!" I said.

"Give it back and I'll bin it" he said.

"I'll bin it myself" I said. As I followed Sandy out of the cook house, I held my plate of mess away from my eyes and nostrils.

On the way back to our billet, I broke away from Sandy towards the NAAFI. It didn't officially open until lunch time, but the cleaners were there, and I entered with my offending plate. A squaddie in fatigues was supervising some local Arab guys to clean up from the night before.

Looking at my plate of mess, he asked "what's that?"

"My breakfast" I replied.

"Ah wouldn't eat that" he said.

"And I'm not going to" I said. He gave me a cleaning bag from a NAAFI bin to put it in. I walked over to one of the vending machines, had a bar of chocolate and a can of coke for my breakfast, then I left with plate in bag for the barrack room.

Sandy was getting ready for bed. We both surveyed at arm's length the so-called mashed potatoes and cabbage. First of all they weren't mashed potatoes. They were SMASH, a powdered form of potato that was mixed with water, in this case to give a consistency of wall paste. It didn't look like mashed potato, it didn't smell like mashed potato, and it certainly wouldn't taste like mashed potato. I sealed it into its bag and stuck it in my bedside locker, got into bed and fell asleep. I awakened at 5 p.m., ravenous for my dinner. I left the breakfast offering in its bag in my locker.

Next morning, washed shaved and dressed, I removed the sealed bag and plate from the locker. From the pungent smell, I could tell that the contents had matured nicely in the heat of the night. At the Branch my mates were looking at me as though I had body odour. I placed my package down on the SSM's desk, and removed the plate of stinking stuff from its bag.

The SSM recoiled, his face purpled and he shouted "for Christ's sake, Private Nelson, get that foul stuff off my desk and into a bin as far from this office as possible!"

"That's what they offered me for my breakfast, yesterday morning, after night duty, sir!"

"They did, sir" said Sandy.

The SSM was fanning himself with a copy of Company Orders. I could see that he was furious. "Get..it..out.. of..here!"

I picked it up and made off outside, to the relief of everyone in the Branch. I made my way to the cook house, where I found a cook house Sergeant overseeing the emptying of the bins. I removed the bag and stuck the plate under the Sergeant's nose. He recoiled a few feet and looked as if he was about to explode. Before he did, I explained that this was what his cooks had offered me for my breakfast yesterday.

"If you'd eaten the fucking stuff then, it wouldn't be in that state now!" he shouted, all the time moving further away. I dumped the lot in one of his un-emptied bins, and returned to the Branch.

There I found all the windows open, which wasn't normally allowed in the heat of an Egyptian day, all the fans going top speed, and the SSM on the phone to the Camp Commandant. Finishing his conversation he turned to me and said, "You should have no breakfast problems from now on" then added, nodding in the direction of my desk "now get on with that pile of typing!"

From then on I had no problem when it was eggs for breakfast. I had a choice of cheese and toast, toasted cheese, or porridge that you could cut with a knife. Much preferable to chocolate and coca-cola.

It was June, and the temperatures were reaching maximum for the year. We were all hot, sweaty, drinking and perspiring hot sweet tea, which unbelievably was the best drink for cooling down and preventing dehydration. Some of us, me included, were suffering from 'prickly heat', which caused an unbearable itch with sweat. We were given 'prickly heat powder' to relieve this, which, when liberally applied to all effected surfaces, had no discernible effect other than to make us look like white ghosts. Prickly heat outlasted my service in the Canal Zone. It embarrassed me for years, brought on when my body suffered a change of temperature, as in stepping from a cold exterior to a hot interior. It was very embarrassing when sitting beside a girlfriend; I was suddenly sweating profusely and desperate to scratch the offending parts. Many a promising friendship was ended by an attack of 'prickly heat'.

Relief from the furnace heat was near. We were now due some 10 days of leave. We had a choice of Army holiday camps at Port Fouad, in the Canal Zone, or Famagusta in Cyprus. Only two of us from the Branch were allowed to go at the same time. Lots were drawn for who would go with whom and when. My friend Sandy and me were drawn first. Sandy was from London and did an imitation of a Scottish accent, or thought he did. We decided to go to Golden Sands Holiday Camp at Famagusta in Cyprus. We thought that being an island in the Mediterranean, it might be somewhat cooler. I was very happy with this decision, because not only was I about to experience another country, my principal reason for wanting to do National Service in the first place, but also my school pal Billy McGregor was serving there in 2 Wireless Regiment. This Regiment specialised in keeping track of Russian submarines and other vessels operating out of Arckhangel, or so Billy claimed. Knowing him, he was probably tuned in most of the time to music on the BBC Forces programme. Anyway, I wrote to him giving him our holiday dates, and he arranged for his leave to coincide. So Sandy, me and another couple of lads from 'G' Intelligence flew out to Nicosia airport in Cyprus. From there we were bussed to Famagusta Golden Sands Holiday Camp. This consisted of tented accommodation along the water's edge, dining hall and Naafi, and several bars and cafes run by local Greeks or Turks. Cyprus at this time was not divided, and the two nationalities cohabited and seemed to get along well enough together. Billy told us that the Turks were more friendly to the Brits, and that the Cypriot Archbishop Makarios, was busy campaigning to have Cyprus ceded to Greece.

Billy had a problem. Apparently Golden Sands was reserved for troops on leave from active service, so it was not possible to reserve a place for him. Some local Greeks looked after the tents, brought tea round every morning, cleaned out the tent and made beds. There were five beds in each tent, so we had an empty bed, but no bedding. British cigarettes were at a premium in Cyprus, where Turkish and Egyptian were the norm. Sandy and me had each been given 100 cigarettes free for the Queen's Coronation. How did the Army Medical Corps allow this? Neither of us smoked, but fortunately Billy, who did, asked us to bring the cigarettes with us, for him. We found a better use for them. 20 Capstan to our personal tent man, provided us with bedding for Billy. 10 a cup of tea for him in the morning, 10 for making up his bed, and another 20 for silence about our intruder. Meals in the camp dining room were 'Cordon Bleu' compared to what we were used to in Moascar. We were issued with a book of tickets, one ticket for each meal. It cost us 50 fags to the dining hall supervisor to obtain one for Billy.

All problems taken care of, the 5 of us settled down to enjoy our exotic holiday. Morning tea, sound of water lapping a few feet from our tent door, early morning swims, afternoon visits to cathedrals built by the Crusaders on high mountains. We savoured the night life of Famagusta and Nicosia. Sitting out in cafes drinking cold beers and hot Turkish coffee till late, buying from vendors with barrows laden with meats, sweets and all sorts of drinks. Open air cinema, the famous Spitfire Club in Nicosia, where fascinated, we watched the belly dancers. We even took part in Greek dancing. What more could one do? A lot.

It was Billy's birthday. What to get him as a present? Someone suggested (it wisnae me) that we have a whip round and buy him a shag. He seemed quite keen on this; like the rest of us he hadn't had one since leaving

Britain, or so he said. We doubted this, as prostitutes, brothels, 'Houses of ill Repute' the Army called them, were legal, and many throughout Cyprus. Inmates of these 'houses' were by law given monthly medicals and certificates of 'cleanliness'. It was much safer having sex in Cyprus than it was in Egypt. A clandestine visit to a brothel there could end up with you buried to your neck in the desert, with your genitals in your eye sockets. Hence the reason that most of us in HQ BTE were chaste. There were local girls in Cyprus that some guys went out with, with honourable intentions. But Billy explained that though a British Serviceman was a great prize for a local Turk or Greek girl, there was a down-side for the soldier. All local girls dating British service-men were accompanied by chaperones, mothers, fathers, or aunties. In cinemas, theatres, cafes, wherever; the chaperone sat between the serviceman and his woman. Any drinks, ice creams etc. had to be bought for the third party too. A Cypriot father didn't mind an evening's chaperoning, when he was having all his drinks at a serviceman's expense. So if you hadn't lost your heart to a local, it was much cheaper to use the professionals. No question of sex otherwise.

For one not used to professional satisfaction, Billy seemed to have a fair idea where such services could be found. Information passed on from an oversexed mate, he assured us. Fortified by several beers and Cyprus brandies, and with Billy's pockets full of free prophylac-tics, we set off. The Army might be against the use of 'Houses of ill Repute', but it was determined not to have its transgressors unfit for duty due to venereal dis-eases, so each Guard House had a box of free sheaths for soldiers to pick up, on booking out for a night on the town. Our first visit was to a house in the old part of Turkish Famagusta. Drunk, amused and excited, we rattled the knocker of a solid wooden blue door. Billy was pressed to the front. It was opened by a woman in her mid thirties, fairly old by our standards then, with a baby at her breast. We could see a man sitting drinking coffee in the dark interior. He gave us a welcoming leer, expecting a large contribution to his brandy bill.

The woman gave us a smile and said, in good English, "I'll be with you when I've finished feeding the baby".

We were aghast at the idea of sex with a woman with a young baby, and an approving husband. We fled down the road, across the ancient stone bridge, built by the Crusaders by the look of it, which linked the Turkish Old Town with the more modern Greek one. We needed a seat at a café, and another couple of brandies before we could muster the courage to continue on our birth-day mission.

Our next house was in the Greek part of the town, a bungalow in a row of neat suburban houses with small front gardens, metal gates and hedges. It could have been any middle class suburb in Britain. We walked up the short path to the front door and rang the bell. Net curtains were pulled back, and my aunt Annie's face looked out: I knew it wasn't her as my last letter from home told me she'd gone to her summer cottage in Balfron. The door was opened onto a long broad hall, pine flooring with a rich red carpet down the centre. The colours were all red and green, like the brothel paintings of Degas and Lautrec (in those days I knew nothing about such artists). What excited us though, was the array of girls, women, ladies in various stages of enticing undress, who lounged around the walls on various chairs and sofas.

Aunt Annie welcomed us in, expecting a good night's takings from us all. She was somewhat taken aback to learn that we only wanted one girl for our comrade. She was further taken aback, annoyed even, that we all accompanied Billy in the selection process. She was furious that we continued window shopping, with no intention of buying, once Billy had disappeared with his choice. I was hit on the back of the head with the Cyprus telephone directory, and decided I'd be safer in the front garden. Opening the door I noticed that on the roadway outside the gate, a Land Rover and a blue van had drawn up. Out of the Land Rover jumped several MPs, and Cypriot police from the van.

I jumped back into the hall, shut the door and locked the Yale. "Military and Cypriot police" I shouted as I ran down the hall to the back of the house. All was chaos. Billy stumbled out of a room pulling on his trousers. The MPs were battering at the front door, and aunt Annie had some trouble releasing the Yale. A topless young girl grabbed me by the arm and pulled me into a room, indicating a wardrobe that I should hide in. The adrenaline rush had cleared my brain of alcohol. I could see me being shut in the wardrobe to be exposed a minute later, her saying "Here's one of them, constable". I pushed my benefactor aside, and jumped for a high open window in the wall. I scrambled onto its ledge and looked down into a walled back garden. It was a scene of noise and confusion. There were MPs, my mates and other clients of aunt Annie, all milling about. The MPs were from the Mauritian MP Regiment, then doing its tour in Cyprus. For MPs they were small, about my size, 5ft 8in; they had handsome regular features, dark hair, and they were wiry and fit. I could see one of them leading away one of our number, and another trying to persuade Billy to come down from the tree in which he'd taken refuge. One was under my window, arms akimbo, waiting to catch me as I came down. I could hear the Cypriot police entering the room behind me, issued in by my would-be saviour. Thoughts were flashing through my mind in split seconds. *What was my granny going to say if I was caught here?* She'd be furious. I looked back into the room; it was the Cypriot police, or the MPs. In the garden the MP was gesturing to me to come down. I jumped into his outstretched arms. He fell over backwards, and I ran for the back wall of the garden.

Sandy, glasses askew, was trying to climb the wall. I pulled myself to the top, and yanked him up. His glasses fell off onto the roadway beneath. We both jumped down, Sandy landing on his glasses. Glasses in those days were made of glass. They were no longer any use to him, so I yanked him away along the road as fast as I could. We ran and ran, breathless, me guiding a half blind man. Street after street, we were aware of dogs barking as we went, we thought they were police dogs chasing us, so we kept running. Eventually exhausted and unable to run anymore, we took shelter in a smelly, unlit public toilet. There we stayed until we got our breath back, and the dog barking had subsided. It was probably only the barking of neighbourhood animals, disturbed in their gardens by our noisy passing.

By the time we left there it was about midnight. We had no idea where we were; we just kept on walking, apprehensive about coming across MPs or policemen. We'd tidied up our appearance a bit, but we still had tears in our civvies from our encounter with the wall. Eventually we came upon a taxi rank, and inquired of a driver if he knew the way (because we didn't) to Golden Sands Holiday Camp. He did, and we settled with great relief into the most comfortable back seats of a car that we'd ever been in. Judging by the time the journey took, the driver took us back via Paphos, to the west of the island, Golden Sands being on the eastern side. We were just so relieved to get out at the camp gate, that we paid his exorbitant price without protest.

The camp guard looked at our dishevelled appearance, gave us a grin, and said "Had a good night then, lads?"

"Great" we said and hurried off to our tent. We sat in there worrying that our mates, caught by the MPs, would break down under questioning and reveal where they came from, and where we were, in which case we could expect at any moment MPs or police to enter the tent and arrest us. We didn't want to go to sleep and be taken unawares in our beds, so we stayed up and worried. Then I remembered that Billy had half a bottle of brandy under his pillow. As he was no doubt being charged and sentenced to several weeks in the Guard

House, he wouldn't be needing it. So we drank it, and felt immediately more confident about our future. As I got into bed, the myopic Sandy wandered to the door of the tent, looked up at the cloudless starry sky, and in his Cockney Scots declaimed, "It's a braw bricht moonlicht nicht the nicht, ye ken. Och aye"

"Try it in a Scottish accent" I said.

We were awakened next morning by our tea man. "Where are the rest of the lads? Have they gone for an early morning swim?" He asked.

Our alcohol fogged brains were slow with coming up with the answer, "Probably". Risen, dressed and ready for breakfast, we still feared being picked up by the MPs. We imagined them marching into the dining room and yanking us out of the breakfast queue. It didn't happen, and we breakfasted on muesli, toast and marmalade. The latter was a treat, no way you got that back in HQ BTE. Breakfast finished and we hadn't been captured yet. The MPs had probably just started their interrogation of their captives again, so we didn't expect to be taken into custody until nearer lunch time. What should we do until then? We didn't know, and couldn't settle to anything. Sandy decided to report sick to the camp Medical Officer, to see if he could be issued with new spectacles. I went with him; not that he couldn't see to get there, just so that I wouldn't be arrested on my own if I went back to our tent. Maybe if it was too much bother to find us, the MPs would just give up, having more important things to do. After all, they already had three of us, what did they need another two for? We'd only be more paperwork for them.

The camp MO was not like the nice Para Lieutenant we had back at HQ BTE. This MO was a regular officer, and we could see that to him National Servicemen were just a nuisance. Why have such a MO in a Holiday Camp? He wanted to know how, where and when Sandy had lost his glasses. Sandy explained that on one of our trips to the castle on mount Troodos, built by the Crusaders, he'd been looking at the vertiginous drop from one of the walls, when his specs slipped from his nose and fell to the valley several hundred feet below. I could see that this was not being believed, and was not surprised when the MO said "Huh, how unfortunate. Well I can do nothing for you; I don't have optical equipment here".

Looking through an open door into a side room, I could see what looked to me to be optical equipment. The MO continued, "you could try a local optician in town, but of course you'll have to pay for it". Bearing in mind the cost, and the fact that most likely we'd be spending the rest of our holiday in the Guard House, we morosely returned to our tent, fearful that the MPs would be there, waiting for us.

What awaited us there in our tent was Billy and our two comrades. Whole, hearty and grinning all over their faces. They'd just arrived back from a night in the cells. They'd been let off with a stiff warning as to what would happen if they were to be caught in a 'house of ill repute' again. Apparently it was not usual to charge soldiers on leave for their first such offence, provided their arrest involved no violence. But they'd had a bad night sleeping on the cells' hair mattresses, and the frugal guardroom breakfast was not to their taste. They were back too late to breakfast at Golden Sands.

Their early good humour at getting off a charge was beginning to disappear, when Billy remembered, "Hey, I've a bottle of brandy here; we can all celebrate with it". They all brightened up at that, and I had a horrible sinking feeling. Sandy disappeared out of the tent, leaving me to explain and reimburse Billy. It crossed my mind that Sandy, Londoner that he was, was leaving me, whom he'd always alluded to as the 'generic tight Scot', to foot the bill. I was not pleased. Deflated we sat around for some time, debating the chance of making the NAAFI before lunch for a wee drink.

After about half an hour Sandy re-appeared again, carrying a bottle of brandy. He'd bought it in the NAAFI. I felt ashamed of my former thoughts, but cheered up as Sandy said, "Och aye, we kin aw hiv a wee dram no". Billy and me looked at each other. I was used to Sandy's attempts at a Scots accent, but Billy wasn't.

"That's a lovely wee accent you've got there" Billy said. "What is it, Welsh or what?"

Holiday over, the SSM welcomed us back to the Branch. He was relieved that the Cornishman and others were going off for their turn at Golden Sands, and that he'd got his favoured typists and clerks back. His preferences were purely professional. Sandy he certainly related to better than me, though it was me that got to do his most demanding tasks. There were plenty of them, holiday time was past. The Sergeant in charge of the Signal

Message Centre had finished his tour of duty in Egypt so he and his family were going back to Britain. That was one less baby-sitting opportunity for us all. There appeared to be no immediate replacement, so the Staff Sergeant who was the SSM's deputy took over. Other duties meant he was not always available.

With bad grace the SSM appointed me to stand in for him on such occasions. "It's a Sergeant's job, Private Nelson, but you're going home in September, so there's no chance you'll be made up to one" he said with relish. "We might manage Corporal, certainly Lance Corporal, if you keep your nose clean". He obviously thought that I might not. "Remember, you signed the Official Secrets Act." I did remember; we'd all signed it on entering 'G' Branch.

The Signal Message Centre was a small room where all the sorting was done of mail, signals and phone calls that arrived in 'G' Branch. There was a small security window on the wall onto the central courtyard around which the various Branches, Intelligence, Training and Operations were grouped. The job consisted of sorting all the stuff that had come in during the morning and previous night, and allocating it to its various recipients. Internal mail was disposed of within the Branch, and external stuff to the Camp Commander, Guardroom or Provost Marshal, was collected by themselves. It was important that whoever was running the Centre correctly assigned the material, so that information that could be anything from 'Restricted' to 'Top Secret' was not sent to the wrong person. Persons collecting had to have proof of identity, usually a pay-book and chit from their Officer Commanding. On my turn of duty, for the first few weeks the SSM or Duty Officer was always in the vicinity to see that I did everything correctly. This annoyed me.

The Signal Message Centre, unlike typing for the SSM, gave one a great overview of all that was happening in the Canal Zone. I loved it. Most of the stuff was boring reports on the cutting of oil pipe lines by the Arabs. But this information had to be quickly passed to our Colonel, who would organise swift action from the Army units in the area of the cuts, and keep the General informed. The General was always making alterations to a Top Secret file called 'Rodeo'. This was his contingency plan for British reaction to anyone taking over the Suez Canal. The British looked upon it as theirs. Colonel Nasser didn't of course, and took it over two years later. The Yanks put a stop to Operation Rodeo, so all my typed amendments were a waste of time.

The messages I liked however, were often delivered by dispatch riders from the various regimental commands in the Canal Zone. These were usually reports to the Provost Marshall of soldiers who were being Court Martialled by their units. Some of these made for delicious voyeuristic reading. A Private Noble of the HLI was being Court Martialled for felling the Officer of the Guard, who had remonstrated with him for being drunk and disorderly on parade. Noble by name, ignoble by nature. I knew Noble well. In the first year at Whitehill Public School he'd walked around the playground with a small wooden ball on a cord concealed up his sleeve. You'd be talking to your pals when you'd receive a very painful smack on the back of your head. You'd turn to see Noble walking off, evidence retracted up his sleeve, and an innocent smile on his face. After one such painful experience I took out insurance of it ever happening to me again. I was the class artist. I spent my time during boring lessons drawing the Spitfires of 602 (City of Glasgow) squadron shooting down Nazi planes bombing the Clyde shipyards. Seeing my proficiency, Noble asked me to draw him some nude women. To avoid further painful taps on the head, I agreed. At 13 my sole anatomical resource for the female figure were the nudes in Billy McGregor's big brother's much fingered copy of the Naturalist 'Health and Efficiency' quarterly magazine. So my nude women had big tits and no pubic hair. The Naturalists weren't THAT keen on nature.

For felling the officer, he was given 6 months in the Glass House, to be added onto his 2 years service, and a dishonourable discharge. I met him in Glasgow a few years later. After a few preliminary remarks to renew our acquaintance, I asked him what he was doing now. He was working as a tailor, cutting suit patterns for a reputable gents outfitter in the city. I couldn't imagine Noble being douce enough for such work.

The HLI had its fair share of Provost Marshal reports. The two 'Buddies' from Paisley, the tall skinny one with whom I'd had the wrestling match, and his short fat pal had disappeared a few weeks ago from our barrack room. No one knew where they'd gone. Two Regimental Policemen had arrived to take all their stuff away; that was all we knew. They'd been an odd pair, and never really integrated with the rest of us. I read this Provost Marshal report, and knew then what had happened to them. Apparently they'd gone into Fayed with their kilts on. After a morning's drinking they'd settled themselves down on the steps leading to Fayed Post Office. Regularly every afternoon a party of Christian Sisters led a crocodile of Convent girls past the post office to prayers. As the young girls passed, the pair stood up, lifted their kilts and waggled their genitalia. One of the sisters ran past them into the post office and called the MPs. When charged they pleaded that they hadn't realised they didn't have their underpants on.

By now it was the height of summer, very hot and exhausting, whether you were on or off duty. On really hot nights we took our beds out onto our second floor balcony in order to maximise any breeze available. Those downstairs did the same. At the weekend, when there was no morning inspection and it was very hot, we tended to leave them out there, and sit or lie on them, eating sleeping, drinking, talking. Items of clothing which we'd washed personally, such as singlets and socks were strung up at the edge of the balcony to dry. One afternoon, after being on night duty I was sleeping when I was awakened by laughter coming from the edge of the balcony. I wasn't pleased at being awakened, but I could see that two or three of the guys were leaning over the stone balcony wall, and appeared to be having some sort of game with the guys downstairs. I went over to see what was happening. They had a length of cord onto the end of which they'd made a hook out of a wire coat-hanger. This was being used with varying success, to fish up socks and vests hanging on the clothes line of the downstairs balcony. There was laughter from our guys and swearing from those below, as they saw the occasional sock being hoisted above. The swearing below ceased, and a long thin bamboo pole appeared which successfully removed one or two of our garments, depositing them, recently washed, on the sand of the road below. Our guys didn't find this quite so funny.

As we hung over the balcony trying to out-hook the squad below, a wee rat with beady eyes, a long nose and wispy whiskers claiming to be a moustache, appeared at our side. It had come up with a mouse mate from downstairs, and was wearing two very white stripes on its sleeves. "Right you lot, you are on a charge for the theft of Army clothing, damage to Army clothing, and conduct detrimental to good order and Military Discipline".

We all thought he was kidding at first, but from the look on his face, we realised he had no sense of humour. Originally a National Serviceman, the shilpit one had signed on for 3 years, and was now bitterly regretting it. "This is a game" we said. "Look, the ground floor are joining in".

"No they're not" he said, and sure enough, realising that their pet rat had gone upstairs to sort us out, their pole had disappeared and they had gone quiet. We all tried to reason with him but to no avail. He demanded the names and pay-books as evidence of the names, of the 3 of us. He formerly charged us, including me, despite the others telling him that I'd just got off my bed to join them. I was incensed, as were the others, including those who hadn't been near the scene of the 'theft'. He was hissed as he left the room. He couldn't charge 20 of us. There was great discussion as to what we should do about this. Some thought that a charge would not be brought; rat face, on returning below, would realise that it was a game, and that that would be the end it. It wasn't. Passing by the guardroom two days later, one of our roommates noted that the 3 of us were on Company Orders for next week, charged with theft, damage to Army property and conduct detrimental to Good Order and Military Discipline.

There was further debate in the room about what we should do about this charge of "theft'. To all of us it seemed so ridiculous that an obvious silly game should be turned into something so serious. It was serious if the Camp Commander found us guilty. Then theft would go into our Army records, and we thought, might even be passed onto the civil police. A police record for theft was not something any of us wanted. We weren't even sure whether theft was a regimental offence or worse still, a Court Martial one. Our fears were growing by the minute. If a Court Martial offence, we could be facing 6 months in the Glass House. Court Martial sentences were added onto National Service time served. By the time this charge reached the Provost Marshal, we could be looking at an extra 6 months in the Army. Was I going to be reading my own case passing through the Signal Message Centre? My granny was not going to be pleased about this. Those not directly concerned with the charge tried to reassure us that the charge would be dismissed by the Commanding Officer. We were not reassured.

I decided to talk the matter over with our SSM. Once I'd explained to him that our little game had led to a charge of theft, he considered thoughtfully for a minute and said helpfully "Oh, that is serious".

I'd a feeling he was thinking forward to our possible convictions, and him being left with the Cornishman for typing, and Signal Message Centre Duties. Persisting to get some helpful suggestion from him, I said "What would be your advice then, sir?"

"Leave it with me" he said "and I'll talk it over with my Staff Sergeant".

This was not the immediate help that I was looking for, and did little to relieve me, or my mates' worries. There were only 5 days to go before we appeared on Company Orders. This was much more important than a charge of throttling a 'haggis' name caller, and would not be mitigated by me having a judge and jury of fellow Scots.

I decided to gather our friendly witnesses together, and get them to sign a paper that I would draft, pointing out that the theft was a game, a silly game we now recognised, thanks to the charges laid by the kind Corporal, and that it would never be repeated. This Ronnie Ross, Ray, Sandy and myself hawked around both barrack rooms, and we got about 50 signatures to it. This took several days, and in the midst of it, the SSM called me in. He had discussed the case with his Staff Sergeant, and they had, he told me, come to the conclusion that our best bet was to get all the witnesses to sign a statement to the effect that it was a game, and that no damage was done to Army property.

This relieved us of a great deal of worry, as we'd pre-empted this advice. He also added to our satisfaction, "Staff and I will also give a testimonial on your behalf, saying that up to the present all of you have been exemplary soldiers". To our annoyance, because we realised he was doing this for his own comfort, he added "and how the Branch cannot afford to lose your services for any length of time".

"Thank you, sir" I said. "That will be very helpful, and we will put your suggestion of collecting witness signatures into effect immediately".

The afternoon before our appearance on Orders, I showed to the SSM and his Staff Sergeant my paper defending our conduct on the day of the charge, with the appended witness signatures. They looked at it, whispered to each other, then announced, "You should have had individual statements from each of your witnesses". Our gloom and doom returned. There was no time to get that now. A long period in the Guard House now looked certain, if not a referral to the Provost Marshal for Court Martial. An extra 6 months of National Service in the Glass House, was a possibility. We worried away a sleepless night.

We were marched into the Commanding Officer's office, between 4 Regimental Policemen. We had been relieved by the RPs of our belts and berets. There was history of the heavy web belts with brass fittings, being used as weapons to attack judge and jury, as the Camp Commander and Regimental Sergeant Major were. But the beret? I suppose it had a heavy metal badge, which if the beret were used as a discus, this could be harmful to the recipient. Major MacDonald sat behind his desk, with the RSM standing by his side. The Major was wearing his Argyll kilt, and the RSM the tartan trews of the Royal Scots. This was a solemn affair, not just for us.

The rat faced Corporal was brought in, and read out the charges. I noticed he'd tried to smarten himself up for the occasion, pressed his uniform and blancoed white his two stripes. Then his witness was marched in, and dutifully distorted the facts of the case. The Camp Commander asked who would speak for us. I stepped forward, followed by my RP. I said my piece about it only being a game, in retrospect one that we now realised, thanks to the Corporal, was a silly one, which would certainly not happen again. I stressed that no Army property had been harmed. I handed over my petition with its signatures.

The Major studied it, then said "Sergeant Major, check out half a dozen of these signatures". MacDonald then picked up another paper from his desk and read it to himself. "Hmm.. I see the 3 of you have been given a good testimonial by your SSM and Staff". The Major then had a whispered conversation with the RSM. Then he said to us "The RSM will check out some of your witnesses, and when I consider I have all the relevant information, I'll have you back here for my verdict, dismissed".

We clicked our heels in salute, and were marched out by the RPs. Handed back our belts and berets, we were told by the RP Sergeant to "fuck off now, you barrack room lawyer bastards". Fuck off we did, but I did notice that we left a glum-faced rat behind, with an apology for a moustache droopier than usual.

The next couple of days were fretful, wondering how much time we would have to spend in the Guard House, if we were found guilty. At least the threat of a Court Martial had evaporated, and with it the prospect of an extended period of National Service. We were grateful for that, but still apprehensive, waiting for the re-call by the Regimental Police. The SSM and Staff in the Branch didn't help either. It was obvious that the SSM was getting as much work out of us as possible, in case we were to be unavailable for some time to come. It appeared from his attitude that he considered the latter a distinct possibility. So did we. Bastard rat-faced Corporal. If we ever met him in civvy street...

The Regimental Police arrived at day-break. They marched us down to breakfast, and then to the Guard House, where we once again surrendered belts and berets. We were held in the Guard House for about an hour. At a phone call from the Camp Commander we were marched back into his office. Case dismissed. A dire warning was given as to what would happen to us if we were ever on Orders again. Heels clicked, marched out, given our belts and berets back.

As I made my way from the Guard House I was stopped by an angry RSM. "Private Nelson, you'd have saved us a lot of bother if you had provided me with your list of witnesses first".

"Sorry, sir. I'll remember that for the future".

"Private Nelson, there had better not be a future".

"No sir, certainly not sir" I said smiling, as I had just caught sight of rat face, leaving the Guard House with a disconsolate face, and now only one stripe on each arm.

Back at the Branch, there was rejoicing with our mates, promises of celebratory drinks in the NAAFI at night, and obvious relief from the SSM and the Staff. The former said "Private Nelson, you've a pile of sorting to do in the Signal Message Centre", this with a withering look at the Cornishman. That evening we had a great celebration of our salvation in the NAAFI, cheerfully spending a month's wages on drinks for our witnesses. Corporal (now Lance Corporal) rat's tame mouse kept well away from the NAAFI that night, and us from then on.

My pal Ray Sexton was now a Corporal. We were both on night duty at the Branch. As usual there was a race on entry, to sit in the SSM's chair behind his desk. The winner had the use of the comfiest chair, the phones at his elbow, and a dominant position in the room. So if the duty officer called in of a night, he tended to look to you as the lead duty clerk. Obviously this would not be assumed if there was a Corporal on duty with you. Nevertheless, I wanted the chair and pushed Ray aside to get to it, to no avail. Ray was a large rugby playing type, and his return shove knocked me into the SSM's filing cabinet. One of the drawers slid out, so I pushed it back in. Obviously the SSM had forgotten to lock the cabinet. I decided to have a look inside, see what secrets he kept there, despite Corporal Ray's reminder that this was something that we shouldn't do.

The top drawer was all about records and expenses for the Warrant Officers' Mess. The second drawer contained various manuals on training, weapons and supplies. The third drawer was gold, personal records. Even Corporal Ray wanted to see his personal file. We lifted them out. I read:

'Private Nelson: In Intelligence Tests and Staff Clerical Practice exams, this soldier had excellent results. This, combined with his smart appearance and good parade ground performance, made him a candidate for Officer Training. On his WOSB (War Office Selection Board) interview, he did however, not come up to the standard we would expect of an officer. He did not appear to fully understand the necessity for officers to follow orders to the letter, and if necessary question commands afterwards'.

On reading this there came to my mind some of the messages from General Festing, Officer Commanding HQ BTE, that had passed through my hands in the Signal Message Centre. When Army convoys were fired upon, when passing through Egyptian encampments, which were often only a collection of mud and straw built huts, the Pioneer Corps were ordered in to bulldoze these encampments to the ground. These were the homes of poor Egyptian families. This practise, however operationally desirable, left families in the desert without homes. The Army offered them tents elsewhere, off route of the Army's convoys. But I was appalled at this treatment of the poorest of Egyptian families. As an officer I would have been reluctant to follow such orders. So I had no complaints with the summoning up, that:

'We therefore conclude that Private Nelson is not officer material'.

There was a later hand-written note underneath this, to the effect that I had been put forward for promotion to Lance Corporal by Captain Scott, and Major Malcolm in charge of Training, with a view to later becoming full Corporal. A later note that this was now under consideration. I thought, *this will not come about, after being on Company Orders charged with theft, even though the verdict was 'not guilty'*. My signed list of witnesses at the trial probably marked me down as a 'barrack room lawyer', an infidel to the Army hierarchy.

Ray's personal record was all that a good soldier, promoted to Corporal, should be, though I consoled myself, he had not done as well as me in the exams. I remembered a saying of my father 'it's not what you know, it's who you know that counts'. In Army parlance I think that that can be altered to 'who best knows how to treat their superiors'. We decided that we should not keep this opportunity to ourselves, but share it with our immediate mates. So I jumped on the camp bike and made for the bar at the NAAFI, where I knew our pals would be found of an evening. Three or four of them hurried round to the Branch, and while we placed guards back and front of the office, to warn of unexpected visits-by the SSM or Orderly Officer, the rest examined their records. We had not extended an invitation to the Cornishman, as we didn't think it would be good for him to see his own record. As it was, there was great hilarity as we all read out for general consumption the choice bits from our files. Luckily it was a quiet night's duty in terms of reports of oil pipe line cuts, and we were able to enjoy a beer or two, that the NAAFI lot had brought with them. This was strictly against Branch Orders for duty clerks. So once the revellers had gone, Ray and me had to suck a lot of peppermints as we put the files back in the drawers, shut the drawers and tidied up the room, ready for any visits from authority.

We hadn't many days to mark off on our demob calendars when a new draft of 'pinkos' arrived in the camp. Several of them appeared as our replacements in the Branch. Pink faced and eager, they had to be shown the job by us. Tricks were played on them for our amusement, as had been done to us, on our arrival 19 months earlier. They soon got the idea that they did not have to ask the Cornishman for permission to go to the lavatory. Or that the Staff Sergeant liked to be asked every morning how he had spent the night before. Or that the SSM liked his chair to have a cushion on it which made an unpleasant noise when he sat down.

One morning the SSM gave us the great news that in one week's time, we were being flown back to Aldershot for demob, one week earlier than expected. This caused great excitement amongst us all. There was a sudden flurry of activity in the afternoons after work, where before there was only lassitude. We all had this desire to take back with us, for ourselves, friends and family, things that would mark our service in Egypt. So we visited the shops and flea market in Fayed, there to look for those articles that signified the Arabic experience. Leather photograph albums embossed with pictures of the pyramids, hookah pipes, tapestries with crude pictures of the Sphinx, heavy wooden jewel boxes in sandalwood, studded with fake stones, all designed to deliver the Orient to the Occident. We bought large cream-coloured leather cases, very attractive to look at, very cheap, and very Egyptian looking. They were heavy even when empty. We filled them with our purchases, and our personal clothing. Then we could hardly lift them. Army clothing and equipment went into kit bags. We were all ready to go several days in advance.

We were given our Discharge Books, which informed us of our posting to Army Emergency Reserve units on demob. There was no getting away from the Army. There was also a short Testimonial. Apparently I had provided 'neat accurate work' and 'responded well to responsibility'. The Major who had forgotten the Army Rifle Shoot medals, also noted that I 'could take charge of a situation' or 'small organisation'. The same man whom I'd mislead about the spelling of 'pigeon' said that he had 'always found me reliable'. I was 'neat' in myself, and seemed to get along well with my 'fellows. So there it was, 19 months summed up in half a dozen lines.

We had a whip round to buy something for the SSM and the Staff Sergeant, as a thank you for their testimonial on our behalf, when we appeared on Company Orders. I went into the Moascar book shop and bought the SSM 'The Complete E.G. Wodehouse'. Somebody else bought the Staff Sergeant a personalised (it had his name 'James' etched on it) Pint Beer mug. The Cornishman, who was staying on for another year, was given a copy of 'Agricultural Farming in the UK'. Farming with his father must have been pretty horrific for him, to have signed on in the Army for another year. I think most of us had enjoyed our National Service, but 2 years was enough.

Two days later two Army lorries arrived, we were loaded into one, and our kit-bags and cases into the other, and off we went to Fayed RAF station, cheered off by those left behind. Did the SSM, the Staff, and the Cornishman have a tear in their eyes? No they didn't. We were all excitedly looking forward to the flight home, the lovely civilian Hermes airliner which had brought us here; the lovely female hostesses and their cups of coffee, alcohol, nice food and long legs.

Bollocks. What was this? It looked like a converted World War II York bomber. It was. Seats had been placed inside the fuselage, the floor of which sagged down like a pregnant dog's belly. The fabric of the seats was well-worn and split in places; they were obviously a second hand purchase from British Airways. Sitting up at the back, near the tail, was like sitting in a tatty cinema; you could see over the heads of everyone in front. There was no neat, clean overhead cupboards for hand luggage, that lovely stewardesses enticingly leaned over you to shut before takeoff. All the non-hand luggage, kit-bags and cases had been piled up, and netted for 'safety', behind the pilot's door. Two morose aircraftsmen told us to fasten our seat belts, and said that "No, there was no alcohol available. But we could buy coffee, tea and sandwiches once we were in flight". The engines coughed, spluttered and wheezed into life, the plane shuddered violently, did a fast wobble down the runway, then amazingly took off. The cabin wasn't pressurized, so we didn't go above 10,000 feet. The noise was abominable, but at least we were on our way back home. Or so we thought.

We landed at RAF Malta. Something was wrong with an engine - what a surprise. We were all taken off the plane, no luggage, all the kit-bags and cases remained on board. We were taken into the RAF NAAFI building at the side of the runway, a ramshackle wooden hut, but with nice local girls who giggled away, and handed out cups of coffee and Penguin biscuits. There was no alcohol. There was a juke box there, so we played tunes and drunk the coffee, and tried to chat up the girls, with little success. After about an hour and a half, when we had played all the tunes, drunk too much coffee, and were making no progress with the girls, an RAF officer came in with the news that the engine needed a new part delivered from Britain. We'd be a few days in Malta, and would be transferred to accommodation in the nearby town of Rabat.

Groans went up. "Could we get all our stuff off the plane?" All we had was small packs containing tooth brush and shaving kit, and changes of underpants. The answer was no we couldn't, we'd have to manage for the next few days. Necessities could be bought in Rabat. We were all loaded onto a local battered Albion bus, with a cigar-smoking driver with a face lined and coloured like a prune. He drove like a maniac along roads narrow and twisting, such as they have in the Highlands north of Inverness. Only there they have passing places for oncoming vehicles. As far as we could see, here they had none. We were flung forward as prune face braked fiercely on entering a corner, and flung to the side as he swayed the bus round them. We finally arrived at what looked like a deserted primary school. The driver, still with cigar clenched between his teeth, got out and took up a position at the door. Thankful for our arrival in one piece, we tipped him the few ackers we'd left from Egypt.

We were met by an Army Sergeant who showed us to our quarters. It was a large school assembly hall, which had steel frame beds and hair mattresses arranged around the walls. We then had to collect blankets and pillows from another part of the building. Here we ate and slept for the next two nights. Food was delivered by an Army Catering Corps unit from the capital, Valletta. There was nothing much to do for the next few days. Rabat was a sleepy little town, so we risked the journey to Valletta in the afternoons. In Valletta we visited cafes and pubs, and enjoyed the fresher air of a sea port. We visited another open air cinema, where we groaned and cat-called a showing of how the American GIs had won World War II in Europe. We exited the cinema at 11 p.m. on a hot night, to find a town still alive with activities. Shops were open, the streets were alive with people. We had the most delicious pork sandwiches served to us with a cold beer, by a large jovial local in a butcher's apron, from his stall at the corner of a building. We'd never experienced luxuries like this before. Not in Egypt on active service, and certainly not in rainy up-tight Britain, with its censored cinema, no cafes, and pubs shutting at 9.30 of an evening. On our return around 1.30 a.m., the scary bus service was off. We had the luxury of taxis back to the school. Their driving wasn't much better, but their seats were more comfortable, and after a few beers, we didn't fear so much for our lives. After such a nice night, the Duty Sergeant's annoyance at our late arrival back was of no consequence.

Two days later we were back on the plane, most of us clutching further mementos from Malta. The new engine part didn't seem to improve the performance. The plane still shoogled alarmingly on takeoff and in flight. Looking out of the port holes, we were not reassured to notice a slight up and down movement of the wings. This was not comforting to notice, so we tried to concentrate on the interior, reading, playing cards or sleeping, the latter being difficult due to the abominable noise of the engines. We eventually landed at RAF Stansted, a World War II airport fallen on hard times. We got off the plane to a light drizzle of rain, very sweet and refreshing after the stifling heat of Egypt. We loved it, for a couple of days anyway.

We were bussed back to Aldershot, where 2 years ago it had all began. We saw it with new eyes now, those of seasoned soldiers back from active service and danger in a foreign land. We now had some credibility with those servicemen who had never been in danger, or out of Britain. We hopefully looked for Substantive Bastard Corporal Smith; he was either in hiding or demobbed, so luckily for him and us, we never found him.

Being back in the civilian world took a bit of getting used to. In the Army everything, from rising, meals, work and sleeping went to a strict timetable. All you had to think about was how to fill in the time in between. Civilian life demanded that you organised all this for yourself. I went back to being a stockbroker's clerk, a job with a lot of money and plenty of boredom. My grandparents welcomed me back with a surprise. Knowing that they were living on state pensions, I'd sent them each month a contribution from my Army pay. They hadn't used this as I'd intended them to, but put it into a bank account, which they presented to me on my return. I was quite emotional in thinking how they had deprived themselves of this money for my benefit, despite my treating them so badly over their concerns as to my fitness for the Army.

My granny, who from her 50's, had suffered from rheumatoid arthritis, was now confined to her bed. She had to be nursed there by my grandfather. I gave him as much help as I could, making meals, helping her sit up, turning her in her bed, emptying bed pans. I felt that this was some recompense to her, and a salve to my conscience, for giving her so much ingratitude for her attempts to get me out of my National Service. In 1956 The Egyptian dictator Colonel Nasser nationalised the Suez Canal. I was in the Army Reserve, so I waited in trepidation for my call-up papers. They never came, much to my relief, and to my grief, my granny died that year.

I'd met my fiancé again, who appeared delighted to see me. I viewed her through the memory of my less than rapturous reception of her birthday present, that of an

'Episcopalian Hymn Book'. At 23 with hair cut short, a tight-fitting green hat and matching coat, she seemed to me to be rather too settled in her ways for my liking. She took me to see the American evangelist preacher Billy Graham at the St Andrews Halls. She went forward for his blessing and I stayed firmly in my seat. I wasn't taking a blessing unless there was a free holiday to go with it. She took me to a screening for TB, me who had been passed A1 for 2 years in the Army. I supposed that this was to confirm that I was going to be a healthy husband for her. I was okay but she was found to have a shadow on her lung. She took tablets to cure it. I wondered what my future was to be with this woman. When she told me that there was to be no more sex until our wedding night, I knew my future was not going to be with her.

So began the rest of my life. On the whole I had enjoyed my National Service. Some of it was boring, some of it was exciting, some of it was dangerous. But it gave me a confidence in myself that I never had before, and I was to keep that for the rest of my life. Confidence enough to leave the rich future of the Stock Exchange, and live on a grant (helped out at the end of every month by my much-loved granddad) to attend Art School for 4 years. There was no boredom there.

I am indebted to the undernoted people for various reasons.

To Barbara my wife, for correction of spelling mistakes, punctuation, and her patience with my computer limitations. To Conrad my son, for reading and giving advice on how things could be better put. To my cousin Allan Edgar for giving an English teacher's advice on the text. To David Boyle, who took time off from his painting to advise on structure. To Charlie Allan for his information on the problems of the Lee-Enfield to a left hander. Also to Becky Bainbridge and her team at Grosvenor House Publishing for their patience with my in-expertise computer wise, and their great help in putting a cohesive story together. Any remaining textual errors are mine.

GLOSSARY

Blancoing: An Army block substance, usually white or ochre, for use in colouring and cleaning webbing.

Clootie: Piece of cloth, dishcloth, used to wrap a large dumpling in before boiling. (Scots Dict.)

Dhobbying: Dhobi – washerwoman or laundry boy. (English Dict.)

Dirndl: Woman's dress with full skirt colourfully and strikingly patterned, derived from Tyrolean peasant use. (Eng. Dict.)

Douce: Sweet, pleasant, sober respectable. (Scots Dict.)

Plookit: Covered with pimples, spotty. (Scots Dict)

Shilpit: Thin, puny, pinched looking. (Scots Dict.)

Shoogled: Shake, jog, wobble. (Scots Dict.)

Sonsy: Sonsie – comely, attractive, buxom. (Scots Dict.)

Tatties: Potatoes. (Scots Dict.)

Wally close: A tiled close, entrance to a tenement building, considered a sign of social superiority. (Scots Dict.)

9 781786 231147